ANALYSIS

OF

CARDINAL NEWMAN'S

"APOLOGIA PRO VITÂ SUÂ:"

WITH

A GLANCE AT THE HISTORY

OF

POPES, COUNCILS, AND THE CHURCH.

NEW EDITION.

LONDON:

ELLIOT STOCK, 62, PATERNOSTER ROW.

1891

EDITOR'S PREFACE.

———◆———

THE reissue within the last year of Cardinal Newman's *Apologia pro Vitâ Suâ* would in itself be sufficient explanation of the republication of this *Analysis*, for some time out of print. Both writers having passed away, their respective works may be considered apart from any mere question of authorship. But other and more important reasons have induced us, at the present juncture, to offer this volume to the reader.

The movement, which we may be allowed to call the Romeward movement, inaugurated some sixty years ago, has unquestionably spread and taken deeper and firmer root. To one acquainted with Scripture this need be no matter of surprise; nor do we for one moment imagine that this, or any number of such analyses, however powerfully they might be written, could possibly hinder the growth of that vast ecclesiastical system which those Scriptures so plainly foretell.

Many have seen in "the woman" of Rev. xvii., sitting on the "scarlet coloured beast," a true and awful description of a corrupt and powerful ecclesiastical organization, of which the Papacy has ever been the type, and towards which Christendom is rapidly tending, owing to the Romanizing influences of the present day.

To use the words of another* in expounding this very chapter: "The Church,

* *Plain Papers on Prophetic Subjects*, by the late W. Trotter.

be it remembered, though betrothed to Christ, has never yet been married to Him. When, therefore, that which assumes to be the Church forms unholy alliances with the earth's kings, and corrupts and intoxicates the earth's inhabitants, her sin is described, not as the infidelity to her husband of a married woman, but as the unchastity of one who should have kept herself as a chaste virgin for Christ. Jerusalem, which had been married to Jehovah, is always charged by the prophet with adultery. It is not this sin, but fornication, which is charged on Babylon. And whether we regard this her unchaste character— her name, expressive of the attempt at unity and uniformity, on which God wrote confusion—her imperial state, 'arrayed in purple and scarlet colour'—her riches, 'decked with gold and precious stones and pearls'—her enchantments, 'having a golden cup in her hand full of abominations [*idols*, see 1 Kings xi. 5, 7] and filthiness of her fornication'—her effrontery, 'having her name written on her forehead'—whether we consider these things, *or her cruelty, 'drunken with the blood of the saints, and with the blood of the martyrs of Jesus'*—what doubt can there be that she symbolizes that huge system of fraud, violence, idolatry, and persecution, which has for so many centuries, under the name of Christ, held the reins of empire in the Roman earth, and been supported by its resources?"

In view of these things we desire that this warning voice be once more heard, and that many souls be thereby delivered from an influence of more than human strength, which is now making itself felt in every town, village, and parish of our land.

Further, we hesitate not to say that

the grand and glorious truths of the Gospel are obscured and ignored as much by Ritualism as by Romanism.

The shocking immorality of the *Confessional* has been abundantly exposed by others, and this alone should make every right-minded person shrink from such a repulsive institution. But, besides this, it is in its very essence a denial of Christianity.

The immediate effect of that sin-atoning and God-glorifying sacrifice of Christ on the cross was the rending of the veil. Moreover, it was rent in twain from *the top to the bottom* (Mark xv. 38); and what does this signify, if not that it was the act of God Himself? So long as that veil stood unrent, God remained concealed, and the sinner dared not approach into His holy presence—" The Holy Ghost this signifying, that the way into the holiest of all was not yet made manifest,"

&c. (Heb. ix. 8.) But no sooner was that glorious work accomplished than God's own hand rent the veil, and the believer now has "boldness to enter into the Holiest by the blood of Jesus." (Heb. x. 19.)

And what do Romanism and Ritualism attempt? Is it not to stitch up, from the bottom to the top, the veil that God has rent "from the top to the bottom"?

Christianity teaches that Christ "hath once suffered for sins, the Just for the unjust, that He might bring us TO GOD" (1 Peter iii. 18); it teaches us that "through Him [Christ] we both have ACCESS by one Spirit UNTO THE FATHER" (Eph. ii. 18); that in Him [Christ] "we have BOLDNESS and ACCESS WITH CONFIDENCE by the faith of Him" (Eph. iii. 12); that we have "BOLDNESS to enter into the Holiest BY THE BLOOD OF JESUS" (Heb. x. 18); it teaches us that "the worshippers ONCE

PURGED" have "NO MORE CONSCIENCE OF SINS." (Heb. x. 2.)

Now the *Confessional* robs the soul of all this—it places a poor fellow-sinner, as priest, between the soul and God, and would have us believe that the sinner dare not approach to God Himself.

Not long since a small pamphlet, entitled *Peace with God*, came into our hands. It was "a plain guide for the use of members of the Church of England who have little leisure time." Such a title would naturally lead one to expect some mention of the finished work of the Lord Jesus Christ upon the cross as the resting-place of the sin-burdened conscience, and the foundation of the sinner's peace with God. But, not at all!—the poor, distracted soul is exhorted to go to its confessor, "kneel down and think that you are at the feet of Jesus on His cross, and when you see that he is ready to hear you, say,"

&c.   Well, thank God, if these earthly priests are not always "ready to hear" there is a great High Priest, who is passed into the heavens, Jesus, the Son of God, and He, blessed be His name, is always ready, seeing that "He ever liveth to make intercession." "Let us therefore come boldly unto the throne of grace."

We subjoin a few extracts from this pamphlet : "God freely forgives us our sins upon true repentance [it was explained before that *confession* was a part of true repentance], but for the quieting of our conscience, and avoiding all doubtfulness on a matter of such vital importance, we ought to make a special confession of our sins to God *in the presence of a priest* . . . after which *the priest will absolve* us," &c.

"All men are more or less burdened with a troubled conscience, and all should as a general rule go to confession."

" Repent, and confess your sins before it is too late."

" As you were washed from your sins at Holy Baptism, you may be washed again by the Absolution spoken to you in God's name by His priest."

" Take care how you refuse *so great a means of salvation.*"

Then follow prayers, rules for self-examination, lists of sins, &c.

After receiving Absolution, "*if pronounced,*" from which it appears that this is not always the case, the penitent is exhorted to go home, and to " excite within your heart affections of consolation and confidence, *hope* and rejoicing, that God has forgiven your sins." So that even after Absolution has been pronounced, we cannot be sure that God has forgiven! A more complete denial of true Christianity than is contained from cover to cover of this pamphlet could scarcely be conceived.

That "offering of the body of Jesus Christ "ONCE," by which God "HATH PERFECTED FOR EVER" every believer, is entirely ignored; and, in its place, we find an elaborate system of man's invention by means of which the poor soul is kept at a distance from God, the conscience being *relieved without being purged.*

We should not have been surprised at this from the Church of Rome, but what shall we say to such teaching emanating from England herself!

ALFRED H. BURTON.

ANALYSIS

OF

DR. NEWMAN'S

"APOLOGIA PRO VITÂ SUÂ."

———◆———

I HAD no thought of even reading Dr. Newman's *Apologia pro Vitâ suâ.* I know pretty well, in theory and practice, what Romanism is ; and the History of the Popes is open to every one. But the book has been put into my hands by others, and so far pressed upon me ; and I have read it. I cannot say it has won my respect. It has certain charms about it, and the present state of things clothes it with interest. I think it likely to attract and win no small number of minds. There is a seeming candour on the surface, and men's minds are prepared for it, and "*quod volumus facile credimus.*" The circle of university affections is most powerful—formed as they are just when the heart is fresh and growing to manhood — and amiable, and the reference to them is one of the attractive points of Dr. Newman's book, but cannot decide what salvation and the Church of God is. If we penetrate below the surface, I do not think the charm of the book remains. The reader must judge when we shall have examined it together.

The secret of the course of Dr. Newman's mind is this—it is sensuous;* and so is Romanism. He never possessed the truth, nor, in the process he describes, sought it. He had never found rest or peace in his own soul, nor sought it where it is to be found, according to the holiness of God. He sunk into that system where the mind often finds quiet from restless

---

* No reader must confound this with *sensual.*

search after repose, when wearied in judging for itself, but never peace with God. That is positively denied and denounced in the Roman Catholic system. In his search, he was never—and this difference is all-important — on the true ground or principles of true faith at all. These things his book shows.

From the first Oxford influences he came under, he had a horror of Protestantism. I understand that horror. How earnestly, when I was in the state I have referred to elsewhere in these pages, I should have disowned, and did disown, that name. I looked for the Church. Not having peace in my soul, nor knowing yet where peace was, I too, governed by a morbid imagination, thought much of Rome, and its professed sanctity, and catholicity, and antiquity,— not of the possession of divine truth and of Christ myself. Protestantism met none of these feelings, and I was rather a bore to my

clergyman by acting on the rubrics. I
looked out for something more like
reverend antiquity. I was really much in
Dr. Newman's state of mind. But such
a feeling as to Protestantism is shallow,
and little founded on fact. I do not think,
now, that Protestantism has restored the
Church to purity. It did not see, I judge,
the true doctrine of the Church any more
than Dr. Newman. Protestantism occupied itself with the positive evils in doctrine
and practice that pressed upon men's consciences, and did the best it knew how in
raising national churches, so-called. Still,
its nature is misapprehended. As to the
word Protestantism, it came from the act
of several German princes at the second
Diet of Spires. The previous Diet of
Spires had left each prince free in his own
dominions as to religious matters. At the
second, the emperor, having settled matters
with the Pope, succeeded with the legate
in getting this rescinded. Nothing was to

be changed till the general council was held. The principal northern princes and many free cities protested, nor held the recess for valid, as it was passed only by a majority when they had left. Further, on the Continent, half those separated from Rome are not called Protestants, but Reformed. The Lutherans are Protestants.

But the matter lies deeper than all this. It is a past history; but it is well it should be known. Protestantism practically broke out about indulgences. The pope—infallible according to Dr. Newman—the centre of infidelity in fact at that time, when infidelity was the fashion at Rome, had set the sale of indulgences on foot to get money to build St. Peter's. The sale was farmed out, through the Archbishop of Mayence, to the Fuggers; and the well-known Tetzel, in Germany, and Samson, in Switzerland, were the agents for the sale. But of this hereafter.

I do not enter on the sparring between Mr. Kingsley and Dr. Newman. To say the truth, I think it poor and low on both sides. If Mr. K. thinks Dr. N. dishonest, all this shilly-shallying about gentlemen's points of honour is folly. The eternal truth of God is beyond this fencing. If he thought in his heart Dr. N. told the truth, he should not seek to prove that he did not by subsequent writings. If he did not, there is affectation in treating of points of honour. All this is below the dignity and seriousness of an enquiry into God's truth. On the other hand, Dr. N. is vexed and undignified too; his blots, one, two, &c., are poor, and, as I judge, a failure—undignified, and often very poor in reasoning and tone. That he was vexed with being charged with dishonesty, one can conceive; but vexation is a bad counsellor. I say, poor in reasoning. I take an example. What analogy is there between accepting devoutly a false his-

torical statement, and Sir D. Brewster's
dreams of inhabitants in the stars? This
is a very poor come-off. The author of
St. Augustine's life says, with the evident
wish it should be so, that a statement,
historically false, but which has serious
effects on the whole state of mind of him
who believes it, "will not be without effect
on the devout mind," and that "it has been
received as a pious opinion." It is admitted,
that the alleged visit of Peter, which is
to have this effect, is a pretended visit;
but devout minds will be influenced by
what has been received as a pious opinion.
It is "to be kept quite distinct from documentary evidence," but to have its effect.
This Dr. N. tells us is sober. Is it sober
to look for the effect of a confessed lying
legend on the mind, as a pious opinion?
Now the legend has for its object to exalt
St. Peter, and Rome through him. For
this purpose, falsehoods have been told,
and minds encouraged in receiving them;

and it is a pious opinion to believe it, and not without effect. This, Dr. Newman tells us, is a sober judgment, because it is said it is to be kept distinct from documentary and historic proof. That people may have believed it piously, I may admit; but to justify the reception of a confessedly false legend as a pious opinion, saying that it will have its effect on devout minds, I cannot call sober. It is a proof of what Romanists consider devoutness and piety. It proves another thing, how early the Church was deceived by falsehoods; for we are here told, that Innocent I. (A.D. 416) lets us know, that it was then received as a pious opinion, "that St. Peter was instrumental in the conversion of the West generally." We do get, not sobriety, but a specimen of the kind of thing called devoutness and piety. I have mentioned, however, this part of the book only to say, that while I think it poor in reasoning, it is of a character which in detail calls for no remark. What is important is mainly elsewhere, and to that I turn.*

It is written, that there will be a falling away, an apostacy (2 Thess. ii. 3); and, though faith may be answered in arresting judgment, when impending, no efforts of ours will avert finally the predicted evil. This evil will, we are told, have a double character in the course of its development. The form of godliness and denial of its power or religious evil, and open denial of Christianity or infidelity; superstitious idolatrous religiousness, devoid of spiritual truth, and open infidelity.

It is a singular, but providentially a notable fact, that two brothers should be eminently conspicuous in these two forms

* I find, on my return to England, that Dr. Newman has suppressed all this in his second edition. He has judged, I suppose, as I do, or received counsel to that effect. I have judged rightly in not noticing it. But as many most probably will have the edition I had in writing this, and the point itself has its importance, I leave the paragraph as it is.

of evil.   Mr. F. Newman has given his
personal history in his progress to infidelity;
Dr. Newman, in his progress in falling into
popery.   There are some passages almost
literally identical in their form.   The fact, of
course, would have been the same, whoever
it might have been ; but, as striking in its
effect on the mind, two brothers being representatives of the double form of departure
from the truth, is, I repeat, providentially
remarkable.   The more so, as they have
both come forward to account for it, not
by any direct reasoning as to the truth or
falsehood of what they have left or fallen
into ; but, in each case, in the way in
which their minds were filled with it, that
is, by an account of themselves.   Both
have known how to render their books
attractive, and themselves attractive by
them.   Both of them unquestionably able
men, but I do not, for my own part, think
possessed of any depth of moral percep-
tion.   I speak entirely from their respective

works, of course. I do not put them on
a par. I must say I think the low, and
what I must call filthy, insinuations of
Mr. F. Newman, in his *Phases of Faith*,
ought, though but short and occasional, to
have at once condemned the whole book,
and the state of mind of the writer, in
every mind that had a spark of elevation,
any sense of what is of good report, of
what is comely and pure. From such a
reproach Dr. N. is entirely clear; I shall
defer pronouncing any judgment of his
book till I have examined its contents.
One thing is striking in both; they seek
to persuade us by showing, in their respective books, that they were wrong, and had
each of them to give up everything he
held on the points in question. This is
singular. Each of these books shows us
a mind step by step giving up what they
held as true, and finding they were wrong
at each step. This has an air of candour.
But did it lead them to distrust them-

selves ? Quite the contrary. They would have us embrace the conclusions they have come to, and in which they profess to have the greatest confidence, though in every previous step they had found themselves wrong. Mr. F. N. has given up Christianity altogether, and gives us the phases of his discoveries of mistake after mistake given up; Dr. N., the apology for his life, in which he has relinquished, not the general truths of Christianity, no doubt, but all he once held on the particular points in question. It does seem to me that this shows, not confidence in the truth (for what they supposed such they gave up), but the attaching an immense importance to their own views—I am afraid I must say, to themselves, I mean by that, to the processes of their own minds.

I have no doubt that there is a direct action of the enemy of souls in all this— of Satan. On this I do not enlarge; but I am bound to say so. But is it not

singular that I should put forward the dis-
covery of my being wrong in everything
I held, not as a lowly acknowledgment
of error, but seeking thereby confidence
in the conclusion I have arrived at as a
motive to influence other minds, and that
they should be influenced by it, and
attracted to the persons who thus acquaint
the public so very elaborately with all that
has passed, as they tell us, in their minds?
The public, no doubt, likes confidences,
likes secret histories; and here it has
them, and has them very cleverly written
—seemingly very naturally and innocently,
and on topics which are in vogue. It is
admitted behind the scenes in an interesting epoch, and has the actors familiarly
and confidingly brought before it. This,
of course, attracts. We like to be thus
trusted with secrets, to know what has
gone on.

But here I must go a little deeper into
the nature of this disposition to have

secret histories, though I fear I may not please the public if they condescend to read me ; but I must tell the truth, and it bears on the character of these books. Men like to hear the secret history, and learn the progress of what is evil, much more than of what is good.   Take a young man, in the human sense innocent, gradually getting away from what is honourable and pure, making impulsive efforts to recover himself, but still sinking —getting, alas ! gradually degraded, till he arrives at some terrible and fatal end. Men are interested.   The efforts at re-covery cast a halo round the sinking man. His degradation is, comparatively speak-ing, lost sight of.   Pity surrounds his end; we like to know the details.   A young woman, shining in early youth, wickedly and heartlessly seduced, struggling against the engulphing stream for a while, the moral tone of her mind sinking, sorrow often (if innocence be met), with longings of heart that she were back to innocence, but her career still onward in evil, till she sinks in destitution, and shame, and sorrow! There is not merely pity (for that is right in both cases), but man likes to read the process; and the person whose secret history he follows becomes interesting to him. Now let these persons be recovered from their evil, instead of sinking to ruin; will the steps of their recovery be traced with the same interest? Most surely not. Put one or the other in a newspaper, in a pamphlet, and try. I do not say our moral judgment approves this tendency of mind; grace surely will correct it. I speak of the fact.

Such is human nature, such is the public; for the public is human nature locally modified. Suppose Mr. F. W. Newman, or Dr. Newman, were to return, the one to Christianity, the other to scriptural truth, would their phases of return, or the history of their religious recovery, be read with the same interest? I am fully persuaded they would not. Right-minded people would be glad, individuals would trace it with interest. Dr. N.'s present publication might cause the sale of some of that; but no bookseller would undertake an edition of the history of their recovery as he would of their fall. Alas! that it should be so; but the history of their fall away from truth and into evil, that it is that interests. But that is what their history is a history of.

No one questions that at this moment the power of evil is rampant. Its forms are the deceit of Romanism and the insolence of open infidelity. Dr. Newman avows in result that he knows only the one or the other—Catholicism (that is, Papal infallibility) or Atheism; not the truth for himself. (p. 198.)* What is fearful (though the Christian has nothing to fear, far from

* All through the present work the page numbers have reference to Longman's Silver Edition.—ED.

it) is, not that evil is there, but the perfect impotency of existing forms and corporations (I mean, of such as ought, from their position and profession, to stand against it), to resist that evil. This is the sign of approaching judgment, of being given up of God. It was not Satan's power which drove the blessed Lord out of the world. As its occasion, it brought Him into it. But when His disciples could not cast demons out, could not use the power which had come in, then He says, "Faithless and perverse generation, how long shall I be with you? how long shall I suffer you?"

The country is in progress towards these two forms of evil. The national schools in Ireland are founded on the avowed principle that it was a vital defect to have the Scriptures read in them, and this professedly to please the priests. A lay tribunal has decided that clergymen are not bound to hold the Scriptures to be

c

inspired, and that if they do not contra-
vene articles made for another state of the
Church, they may teach anything they
like; that is, that the Church is no
guardian of the truth at all. On the
other hand, when men are subjected to
the stultified fatuity that a red gown is
like the Holy Ghost, there is no way of
meeting such imbecility in public service,*
because there is a rubric attached to the
liturgy, the expression of patience, ill-
advised or not, at the time when men
were emerging from these things, which
permits what was done in the second year
of Edward VI.

Now, it is not the evil I am judging
here. If men like red gowns, I am sorry
they do not instead love to worship God
in spirit and in truth; but what I notice,
what is fatal in its character, is, that while
the word of God is surrendered, and men

---

* Since this was written some little righteous energy (I
would I could say consistency) has been shown by Dr.
Tait, for which I desire to be abundantly thankful.

are judicially authorised to give it up, there is no autonomy, no power, avowedly no power, to stand against or remove evil. The authorities of the national body seek to tide it over with the power of evil; but there is no faithfulness to God; and we have Father Ignatius at the Episcopal gathering as a deacon of the Church of England, and having a right to be there; and we have Colensos and Williamses openly setting aside the word with impunity. Neither can be met, neither can be dealt with as evil. They are authoritatively or judicially accepted; there is no intrinsic power at all to meet evil. I do not doubt the faithfulness of the Lord; I have no fear; I hold it to be a time of great blessing for faith; I believe the Lord is at hand. But it is sorrowful when what, in some sense at least, was the professed seat of righteousness, declares its incapacity to remove or resist evil. If it be so, we are on the

way to judgment. The aristocratic mind
tends to popery; the popular to infidelity.
Ecclesiastical authorities are powerless
against the former; they are the chief
abettors of the latter. Truth remains,
blessed be God, always itself, and grace
cannot fail.

As I have spoken of these two forms
of evil, let me add a few words on them
before I formally take up the book which
has given occasion to these lines. It is,
as regards the true object of these remarks, the best judgment on the book.
I am greatly confirmed in the conviction,
that at the root of Romanism lies infidelity,
not, of course, in the gross form of denying
Christianity in its fundamental truths, or
the historical basis of Christianity, but in
the annulling those truths on which the
blessing of the soul depends, or their
application to it. It is a sensuous religion,
fills the imagination with gorgeous ceremonies, noble buildings, fine music, stately

processions. It feeds it with legends and the poetry of antiquity; but it gives no holy peace to the conscience. Ease it may, but not peace; and while accrediting itself with asceticism,* accepts for the mass of its votaries full association with the world. It holds sin over the conscience as terror, and relieves from that terror by human intervention, so as to put power into man's hand—into the hands of the priesthood. Looked at as a picture, it fills largely the imagination; in practice it degrades. Christianity and (in its true sense, whatever its shortcomings may have been) Protestantism elevate. I shall refer to this last in a moment. It has largely failed in result, but in its nature, as compared with Romanism, it elevates.

Christianity brings us directly, *immediately*, to God. Each individual is directly, immediately, in relationship to God—his

* "I looked at her," says Dr. N., "her rites, her ceremonial, her precepts, and I said, This is a religion."

conscience before God, his heart confidingly in His presence. Judaism had a priesthood, the people could not go into God's presence. They might receive blessings, offer offerings, celebrate God's goodness, have a law to command them ; but the way into the holiest was closed by a veil : " the Holy Ghost this signifying, that the way into the holiest was not yet made manifest." (Heb. ix. 8.)   When the Lord Jesus died, this veil was rent from top to bottom, and "we have boldness to enter into the holiest by the blood of Jesus, by a new and living way which He has consecrated for us through the veil, that is to say, His flesh " (Heb. x. 19, 20); " He has made peace through the blood of His cross" (Col. i. 20); " suffered, the just for the unjust, to bring us to God" (1 Peter iv. 18); His blood cleanses from all sin.   Hence the essence of Christianity as applied to man is, that the Christian goes himself, directly, personally to God, in Christ's name, and through Christ, but himself, into the holiest, and with boldness. He has by Christ access through the one Spirit to the Father, the Spirit of adoption. This being brought nigh by the blood of Jesus characterises Christianity in its nature. The holiness of God's own presence is brought to bear on the soul, "If we walk," it is said, "in the light, as He is the light" (1 John i. 7)— yet not as fear, which repels, for we know perfect love through the gift of Jesus—we have boldness to enter into the holiest, that place where the presence of God Himself assures that the confidence of love will be the adoration of reverence, while we go forth to the world, that the life of Jesus may be made manifest in our mortal body, the epistle (as it is said) of Christ. I am not discussing how far each Christian realizes it, but that is what Christianity practically is. He has made us kings and priests to God and His Father. This elevates truly. Man is not elevated by intellectual pretensions; for he never gets, nor can get, beyond himself. What elevates him is heart-intercourse with what is above him; what truly elevates him is heart-intercourse with God, fellowship (wondrous word!) with the Father, and with his Son Jesus Christ. But, even where the heart has not found its blessed home there through grace, this principle morally elevates; for it at least puts the natural conscience directly before God, and refers the soul, in its estimate of good and evil, personally and immediately to Him. There may be self-will and failure, but the standard of responsibility is preserved for the soul. I do but sketch the great principle on which I insist.

Romanism, wherever it exercises its influence, has closed the veil again. The faithful are not reconciled to God, they cannot go into the holiest, do not know (as they quote from Ecclesiastes with so false an application) love and hatred by all

that is before them ; they have a priesthood and saints and the virgin Mary
between them and God. Christianity is a
divine work which, through the redemption and life of a heavenly Mediator, has
brought us to God ; Romanism, a system
of mediators on earth and in heaven,
placed between us and God, to whom we
are to go, and who go for us ; we are too
unworthy to go ourselves. It sounds lowly,
this voluntary humility, but it shuts out
the conscience from the witness of God's
presence ; it casts us back on our worthi-
ness ; it puts away and denies the perfect
love of God as known to us (shed abroad
in the heart by the Holy Ghost given to
us) through Christ. It repudiates the
blessed tender grace of Jesus, that High
Priest who can be touched with the feeling
of our infirmities ; we must go to the heart
of Jesus through the heart of Mary, they
tell us. Surely I would rather trust His,
blessed and honoured as she may have

been and was in her own place. It removes me from God to connect me immediately with creatures, however exalted, for my heart, and with sinful men for my conscience, who are to judge of and absolve me.

All this is degrading; it is the denial of Christianity, not in its original facts, but in its power and application to man. A few illustrations of what I mean. They hold the great facts or truths of Christianity — the Trinity, the divinity and humanity of Christ, the atonement, so far as its sufficiency goes, (not, however, as effectual substitution,) that men are sinners (this also very imperfectly); and the need of regeneration, though they scorn the true force of the word. They hold the inspiration of the Scriptures, though they have falsified them, both in adding books which every honest man knows are not genuine Scriptures, and giving a translation as the authentic Scriptures. They own in a general way the personality and agency of the Holy Ghost. My object is not here to state exactly every point, but to say in general that they own the great fundamental facts of Christianity. It is not there that the spirit of infidelity shows itself.

But the moment you come to the application of these facts to men—to their efficacious value, all is lost. The Scriptures are inspired, but the faithful are incapable of using them. In vain is it that they are addressed by God Himself through the inspired writers to the body of believers —they must not have them but by leave of others. In vain is it that there is a Holy Ghost; He does not so lead and guide individuals as that they can walk in peace and grace, and understand withal His word. They mock at the thought of His dwelling in believers. They bring the divisions and faults of believers to prove He cannot be there; that is, they use man's sin to deny God's goodness and truth, just as

infidels do.   Even as to the Scriptures
their universal question is the same as the
infidel's—How do you know them to be
the Scriptures?   Their doctrine is, You
must believe in them through the Church;
that is, they do not command faith in and
by themselves, nor is man guilty if he
reject them, just as the infidel says.   God's
word must be believed because God has
spoken, and for no other reason, or it
is not believing *His* word at all.   Grace,
no doubt, is needed for it, as for everything; but man's responsibility is there, as
the Lord said, " If ye believe not that I
am He, ye shall die in your sins."   They
were responsible for not receiving Him,
with all Ecclesiastical authority rejecting
Him : so are men as to the Word.

Again, the sacrifice of Christ, they do
not deny it.   They repeat it in the Mass
in an unbloody sacrifice, they say.   But
Scripture says it was accomplished *once
for all*, and contrasts it in its efficacy with

the Jewish sacrifices, the repetition of
which proved that sin was still there.
Whereas the sacrifice of Christ, offered
once for all, having perfectly put away sin
for him who believes, there could be no
repetition, the believer is perfected for
ever, and God remembers his sins and
iniquities no more. Their repetition shows
unbelief in this blessed truth. The believer
is not perfected for ever—the sacrifice
must be repeated. It is not true that
God will not remember their sins and
iniquities any more. That is, the sacrifice
is not denied ; its efficacy, once offered for
the believer's soul, is.

Again, take Christ's intercessional
mediatorship. Christianity presents to
me that blessed One, in whom dwells
all the fulness of the Godhead bodily,
a man tempted in all points as we are,
without sin ; one who also can be touched
with the feeling of my infirmities, who
has suffered being tempted, and thus is

able to succour them that are tempted. In a word, the Son of God Himself has descended into our sorrows and trials, and passed through them in tender, gracious love that I might confide in His sympathy and love, and know He could feel for and with me.   Do they deny His priesthood and intercession?   No.   But in fact there are a crowd of mediators; above all, Mary His mother.   And why?   He is too high and glorious.   Any poor man would seek a friend at court to have the king's ear; it is the heart of Mary I am to trust, and get the saints' intercession, and get at His heart through Mary's.   The whole truth and value of Christ's intercessory love is destroyed and denied in practice.   The saints and Mary's intercession is trusted, their tenderness and nearness believed in, not Christ's.   Heathenism denied the one true God the Creator (though in a certain sense owning Him as a dogma) by a multiplicity of gods in practice.   God intervenes by a Mediator in the most perfect system of blessing, and Romanism, while admitting the mediatorship of Christ as a dogma, has denied the one true mediatorship in practice by a multiplicity of mediators. It is the heathenism of Christianity, that is, of the blessed truth of a redeeming Mediator.

I turn more immediately to Dr. Newman's book. Let me be forgiven speaking for a moment of myself, as what I say has a bearing on these points. I know the system. I knew it and walked in it years before Dr. Newman, as I learn from his book, thought on the subject; and when Dr. Pusey was not heard of. I fasted in Lent so as to be weak in body at the end of it; ate no meat on week days—nothing till evening on Wednesdays, Fridays, and Saturdays, then a little bread, or nothing; observed strictly the weekly fasts, too. I went to my clergyman always if I wished to take the sacra-

ment, that he might judge of the matter.
I held apostolic succession fully, and the
channels of grace to be there only.   I
held thus Luther and Calvin and their
followers to be outside.   I was not their
judge, but I left them to the uncovenanted
mercies of God.   I searched with earnest
diligence into the evidences of apostolic
succession in England, and just saved
their validity for myself and my conscience.   The union of Church and State
I held to be Babylonish, that the Church
ought to govern itself, and that she was
in bondage, but was the Church.

I would guard this part of what I say.
I still think fasting a useful thing in its
place, if spiritually used.   I still think
there were sacramental ordinances instituted.   I still think the State has nothing
to do with the Church.   Only I add, that
if it be so, the Church must not be an
imperium in imperio, but a lowly heavenly
body, which has no portion on earth at

all ; as it was at the beginning, suffering
as its Head did, unknown and well known,
an unearthly witness of heavenly things
on earth. What saved me then, I think,
from being a Romanist, was the ninth and
tenth of Hebrews. I could not for priesthood, which I believed in, give up practically our great High Priest and His
work. What delivered me from this
whole system was the truth. The word
of God had its own, its divine, authority
over my soul, and maintained it through
grace. I was looking for the true Church
honestly, but in the dark. I believe in
the Church now, but I know it in its
reality only as the living body of Christ
united to Him by the Holy Ghost. I
believe there is a Church on earth, but, as
is prophesied by the apostles, utterly corrupted as an external thing, and ruined,—
" having the form of godliness, but denying the power of it," causing perilous
times. I see the Church, the body of

D

Christ, composed of living members united to Him by the Holy Ghost. I see also an outward system, the habitation of God through the Spirit; but there I see wood, and hay, and stubble, may be built* in, and has been, and worse, but that God's faithfulness will continue His own work. *Christ will build* till all be finished, and no power shall prevail against it, until the time come to take those that are His to glory. I believe the appropriating the privileges of the members of Christ's body, as a fact, to all that are built into the house, is the fundamental principle of popery, and all that clings to it. I admit a sacramental

---

* What Christ builds will be infallibly maintained to the end; and to this Peter refers in 1 Peter ii. But, also, as in every divine dispensation from the beginning, what God had established in a right state has been entrusted to man's responsibility, and man has uniformly failed, and the system has been judged. So of the external system of the Church—the day will declare the work, for it will be revealed by fire. The corruption will be destroyed.

system, but to identify it with actual spiritual power is unscriptural and false; one may be corrupted by man, the other is the work of God, and secured by Him. I know no salvation out of the true Church; but the Roman Catholic Church is ridiculous as a security for the soul; for they admit that men may be, and hundreds are, members of it, and lost after all. I would not thank you for such security as that. I do not think Protestantism was fully delivered from this identifying the external sacramental system with the divine power of life—these two distinct revealed aspects of the Church—and hence its present difficulties. Romanism specifically and as a system identifies them, denies the spiritual power, and regeneration by the Word, and the indwelling of the Holy Ghost; in practice, mocks at it, as an infidel might. It is essential falsehood in this respect. Protestantism does not. It owns the spiritual

power and the Word; but I do not think
there was deliverance from confusion as to
it.   It is bearing the burden of this now.

We are told there shall come a falling
away.   As I have said, I believe it.   The
apostle has declared, that is, God has
declared, " Towards thee [the engrafted
Gentile] goodness, if thou continue in His
goodness; otherwise, thou also shalt be
cut off." (Rom. xi. 22.)   Falling away,
the opposite of continuing in God's goodness, is prophesied of; the lot of the
Church, as an outward professing system,
is to be cut off.   I look for partial present
success for Romanism—the unbelief of
imagination, and especially in its influence
over government—but to make a way for
open apostasy, or infidelity, the instrument
of desolating judgments on it when Antichrist and judgment will close the scene.
Into that system of corruption which shall
thus be destroyed, though for the moment
successful, Dr. Newman has cast himself,

as many others have, out of the uncertainty in which he has found his mind. His brother, as we have seen, publicly represents the open infidelity. Dr. Newman rests on authority; for him the Pope is infallible. I have found (through pure grace, I fully own) the truth deliver me out of all difficulties, and the sure stay of my soul; for the word of God abides for ever. I rest, through grace, on the truth; on divine authority; on apostles, not on the Pope. Dr. Newman cannot say, I know of whom I have learned it. I can. I have learned it of Paul, John, Peter—I need not name the rest — yea, of the blessed Lord Himself.

I will examine the process of Dr. Newman's mind. He has set it before us for the purpose. I pity Dr. Newman; I feel his difficulties; I have felt them myself; I do not judge him. But as his book is calculated to interest and influence many, I do not think he can complain if I dissect it freely. It is impossible to do so without speaking of Dr. Newman himself; for the whole part of his book which I comment on is an account of himself. I must necessarily expose his state in commenting on his own account of it. In many things I agree; many of his thoughts I have gone over in my own mind. Strange to say, I find I admit constantly all that infidels hold metaphysically. Only the truth remains, the truth of God untouched. I account for some of their thoughts; cannot for others. What Dr. Newman calls liberalism is infidelity — man meddling, with his own mind as competent, in divine things. I reject this as utterly as he does. In the two points he professes to name, I do in a measure, I suppose, pretty much as he does; but *he* need not be so afraid of liberalism. What it hates is truth. Its latitudinarianism will favour—is favouring —Popery at present more than anything else does, and has been. I believe the

time will come when it will pull down
Popery. I believe the time will come, as
Dr. Newman says, when a mere *via media*
will disappear as satisfying nobody, and
the struggle will be between Popery and
Infidelity directly. I believe infidel power
will triumph, and Popery disappear; but
triumph to its own destruction by the
judgment of the Lord. But at present
the liberal principle, and the majority of
Dissenters with it, are attacking the Establishment, the *via media*. It stands in their
way. Some have boasted to me of their
doing so, looking for the result Dr. N.
himself anticipates; that is, putting down
the Establishment, and then having a final
struggle with Romanism. I have no sympathy with this in any sense or way. They
are deceiving themselves too. They will
find liberalism too strong for themselves as
a system. What is religious, as a system
among them, will not, does not, satisfy
any active religious or infidel mind now.

They may grow for a time by the ruin of others; but they are letting loose what will ruin themselves. But there is another thing besides and behind what Dr. Newman is looking at—*the truth of God, the people of God.* They will subsist and have their place in heaven when the fashion of this world has passed away.

There will be a people, not liberal so-called, not Romanists, but heavenly, Christian men, resting on the word of God in true and lowly faith, led by the Spirit, kept, whatever the ruin, against whom the gates of hell shall not and never can prevail. They will be kept, I mean, in the world, where alone danger for them is. They will have the sacraments, for such there are; but they will have what is inward and essential—true, divinely-wrought faith, and the Spirit of God; kept by the power of God through faith unto salvation ready to be revealed. May Dr. Newman be found among them, and many of the liberals too ; yea, his now poor infidel brother, for grace can gather from every quarter. I am perfectly assured that the gates of hell shall not prevail against the Church that Christ builds ; and I mean that He will keep it as a public profession here until the moment known to God, when He will take His own to Himself in heaven. But that which man has built and corrupted, the servant which has said, " My Lord delays His coming," and has beaten the men servants and maid servants, and has eaten and drunk with the drunken, will be judged, have his portion with the unbelievers, with the hypocrites, though called His servant to the end. It is well that men who fear God should ponder these things.

The first point which prominently strikes me in Dr. Newman's book is, that, as far as I can find from diligently examining it, neither Christ, nor the truth, nor the

word of God, nor any true solid foundation ever was in his mind at all.   I hasten
to say, I am not speaking of what is called
orthodoxy.   I am assuming that, as he
does.   He professed these great Christian
foundations before; he professes them
now—sincerely, I doubt not, as dogmas
then and now, the useless faith of James.
But in his search on the point which
occupied his mind, in what he discloses
in this book, neither Christ, nor the truth,
nor the word of God, nor any divine
ground of faith, is found as an object
of research, or possessed as the foundation of his soul.   As to a divine foundation
of divine faith, it is from beginning to end
denied.   Romanism has none.   It has
dogmas, immensely important, fundamental
dogmas they are, but no divine ground of
faith.*   My business is here to show that

---

* I do not undervalue these dogmas.   They are
essential to Christianity, and we cannot estimate them
too highly, or hold them too fast.

it is so, as to Dr. N. His enquiry was between Anglicanism and Romanism. The
soundness and fairness of that enquiry
I will speak of; but there are deeper
principles at the bottom of the result he
has arrived at, and to them I now turn.

I affirm that, as far as this book goes,
there is no divine ground of faith at all
in it. He says he was converted at
fifteen. Charity will surely hope and
trust it is so. I do not pretend to judge,
I earnestly hope it is; my heart gladly
believes it, and rejoices in the thought of
it. There is One only who judges. I
speak of his book, and the principles laid
down there. Whether Christ ever appears
there, people must judge of, who have read
it. I cannot recall the instance. And this
is exceedingly important, as to what religion
is. Possessing Christ, having the Son, as
Scripture expresses it, gives a rest and
peace to the soul, which does not leave it
beating about after truth, as Dr. Newman's

was, saying, Where is it? The soul that has Christ knows it *has* the truth—for 'He is it—that it has found the Father. It does not hunger, as not having what the soul needs and craves after. It is not looking about for safety, for it is safe in Him and through Him; not in self-confidence, but trusting the good Shepherd, who knows His sheep, and keeps them. It does not slight the sacraments, but is thankful for them, nor the ministry of men whom the Lord has sent. It blesses God heartily for all these things where it enjoys them, but it possesses the substance of all, eternal life in Christ, shepherd-care in Him. It has peace and rest of heart in Him.

And there is another point connected with this. What finally led Dr. Newman to be satisfied with Romanism, which has confessedly a multitude of doctrines unknown to the primitive Church, was the principle of development. He was far down the hill, no doubt, long before, but

that plunged him into its waters.   Now in
the person of Christ, and the value of His
work before God, there can be no development.   He is the same—and so is the
efficacy of His work—yesterday, to-day,
and for ever.   I or Dr. Newman may
grow in the knowledge of Christ.   Faithful
zeal may resist and dispel errors which
arise, and by which Satan seeks to cloud
the truth and overthrow faith ; but there
cannot be a development of the infinitely
perfect and completely revealed person
of the Son of God, in whom dwelleth all
the fulness of the Godhead bodily.

Dr. Newman may find (in spite of
Bishop Bull, and as Pettau has admitted)
that the ante-Nicene fathers were worse
than obscure as to the divinity of the
blessed Lord; but Paul is not, who declares
that the fulness of the Godhead (θεότης not
θειότης, that is, proper Deity, not divine
character simply) dwells in Him bodily ;
John is not, who declares He is the true

God, was with God, and was God; and the New Testament, so plainly and blessedly making Christ known to us, is not. There He is Immanuel, Jesus,—Jehovah the Saviour. He may rejoice that the Nicene council re-affirmed this truth. But to say that this was development, and that the Church of God *for three centuries* did not know the true divinity of Christ, is high treason against Christ and the truth. It is the folly of a mind which, to excuse itself, and make out a point, gives up all fundamental truth—does not possess it. It may lead to Romanism—I dare say it does; I am sure it does not lead to God. The apostle tells us, on this very head, " Let that therefore abide in you, which ye have heard *from the beginning.* If that which ye have heard from the beginning shall remain in you, ye also shall continue in the Son, and in the Father." (1 John ii. 24.) There might be the rejection of heresies, as Arianism, whose source was in Platonism

and philosophy, or of other similar evil
doctrines; but it was not to develope, but
to maintain what was from the beginning.
So the apostle Paul, " But continue thou
in the things which thou hast learned
. . . knowing of whom thou hast learned
them." I admit no development: that is
Popery.

I admit of no private judgment, when
God has revealed the truth. I will touch
on this subject further when I come to
speak of Dr. N.'s views of Protestantism. I learn, but I know of whom I
learn; I continue in what we have heard
from the beginning. The Romish Church
does not so continue; it does not know
of whom it learns, as to the faith of any
individual in it. The indiscriminate reading
of Scripture by Christians it condemns,
which the apostle gives as the resource
and security of the believer in the last and
evil days. We are perfectly sure why.

Next, it is striking how absolutely

foreign the search for the truth, or the conscious possession of it, was from Dr. N.'s mind. He was looking out for some *via media* to preserve from what threatened. The Evangelical system only occupied a space between Catholic truth and rationalism. (p. 102.) I do not know what else a *via media* of his own was to do. But I refer to this now to show there was no search for God's truth in the matter; it was some expedient. "It was necessary for us to have a positive Church theory erected on a definite basis; this took me to the great Anglican divines." (p. 104.) Then there were the *parties* in the controversy, the Anglican *via media*, and the popular religion of ·Rome. The Anglican disputant took his stand upon Antiquity or Apostolicity, the Roman on Catholicity. (pp. 106–111.) "It is plain, then, that at the end of 1835, or beginning of 1836, I had the whole question before me on which, to my mind, the decision between

the churches depended. . . . There was a
contrariety of claims between the Anglican
and Roman religions, and the history of my
conversion is simply the process of working
it out to a solution." (pp. 111, 112.) It
was Catholicity, or Antiquity. I add that
the unity of the Church, as one body, was
not in his mind at all. It was Catholicity,
or independent dioceses. On reading Leo
he suddenly felt he was all in the wrong.
"Be my soul with the saints," such as
Athanasius (who died excommunicated
and banished by the so-called universal
Church for the truth's sake) and Leo.
"Anathema to a whole tribe of Cranmers,
Ridleys, Latimers, and Jewels! Perish
the names of Bramhall, Ussher, Taylor,
Stillingfleet, and Barrow from the face of
the earth, ere I should do aught but fall
at their feet in love and in worship, whose
image was continually before my eyes,
and whose musical words were ever in my
ears and on my tongue." (p. 116.) Is

there the most distant idea of an approach to the serious search of God's truth on the subject from His teaching? Dr. N. moves in a circle of men's minds to decide a question of the merit of present rival schemes, never for the truth of God. Where he had learnt what he did hold we shall see in the next article. Even here we shall see he rests on no divine testimony. There is no seriousness. Dr. Wiseman's words from St. Augustine, "*Securus judicat orbis terrarum,*" sounded in his ears incessantly, like "Turn again Whittington!" (pp. 116, 117.) "There was more evidence in Antiquity for the necessity of unity, than for the Apostolical succession," etc. The truth of God, as revealed, does not enter his mind. He cannot say he possessed it, or thought he did it; for he was uncertain and changing, and that even as to why he was to believe; but in this state never enquired for God's truth on God's authority.

Again, further on (p. 198), he examines
the concatenation of arguments by which
the mind ascends from its first to its final
religious idea : "And I came to the conclusion that there was no medium in true
philosophy between Atheism and Catholicity, and that a perfectly consistent mind,
under those circumstances in which it finds
itself here below, must embrace either one
or the other." Now, such a sentence could
not by any possibility have been penned by
one who possessed the truth himself. One
who possessed Christ, knew Him as the
Son of God for himself, knew the Father
and His love, must have known that there
was the possession of truth without being
what Dr. N. (when he wrote this) means
by Catholic. No one who possessed
divine truth, as taught of God, whatever
the external means—truth as to God, the
Trinity, the Lord Jesus, the Church as one
with Him, sin, salvation (I might enlarge
the list)—could have declared there was no

medium between Atheism and Catholicity.
And note his grounds : " I am a Catholic
by virtue of my believing in a God; and
if I am asked why I believe in a God, I
answer that it is because I believe in myself." (p. 198.) God's presence in his conscience makes him know God. Now, Dr. N.
speaks of philosophical correctness. It is
not the question here. Either before joining
Rome he *possessed* Christian truth, or he
did not. If he did, his position is false ;
if he did not, any one can understand why
he turned Catholic. He had nothing. Nor,
indeed, did he arrive at anything. He
came to authority, not faith in any truth.
He did not believe, he tells us, in transubstantiation till he was a Catholic. Now
he receives it on authority. (p. 239.) He
believed that the Roman Catholic Church
was the oracle of God. Transubstantiation
passed muster with all the rest, and he
declared it to be a part of the original
revelation ; but this is no true faith in a

truth, it is acquiescence in authority, and, after all, it is accrediting Rome for a fact. I might add to this list of proofs that he did not possess the truth, nor seek it. I quote this only as short expressions of it on his part, and so proofs. The whole book shows it—it runs through every part of it.

I shall now show that he had no divine ground of faith. His whole ground of believing was, not divine testimony, but probability, and no more; and such is the doctrine of the school, as I shall show from Keble. No wonder that Romanism delights in this. It has no divine ground of faith. It cannot give the same ground of faith to a heathen and a Christian, nor any sure one to either. It declares, I cannot believe in God's word but on the authority of the Church. But how am I to believe in the Church? The first converts could not. Antiquity, catholicity, succession, did not exist. They were called on to believe in Christ alone. There was no Church, and all ecclesiastical authority was against Him. The foundation of the first disciples' faith is different on the Romanist system from mine; and, even after Christ was glorified, the faith of the converts could not be founded, and was not founded on the Church, but on the testimony of the apostles. Nor could it be with heathens now; for they do not recognize the Church. It is said that there is special grace for them. So heathens have special grace which Christians cannot have. And if, as believing in Christ, I seek, not Christianity, but honestly what church is the best one, I am told I must begin by owning the authority of that Church. But this is absurd on the face of it; for what I want to know is, Has it authority? Is it the true Church?

I return to the ground Dr. Newman was on. Now, the truth rests on testimony. John the Baptist says, "He that has received His testimony hath set to his seal that God is true." (John iii. 33.) So the apostle John : "He that knoweth God heareth us." (1 John iv. 6.) So Paul : "Continue thou in the things that thou hast learned, knowing of whom thou hast learned them." (2 Tim. iii. 14.) Now, if I believe the blessed Lord's testimony, or Paul's, or John's, or any of the inspired witnesses, I do not, I cannot, dare not speak of probability. I set to my seal that God is *true*. There is no divine faith but that. That Dr. N. never had in prosecuting his inquiry. He tells us so. It was one of the great underlying principles of a great portion of his teaching— "Probability is the guide of life." (p. 19.) The difficulty was evident: scepticism, that is, certainty about nothing. Keble met this, he tells us, by the doctrine, "that it is not merely probability which makes us intellectually certain"—mark, "intellectually."

He had spoken before of the logical co-
gency of faith (p. 11)—"but probability as
it is put to account by faith and love. It
is faith and love which give to probability
a force which it has not in itself." (p. 19.)
Thus in itself it was only a probability,
and something in myself gives it force. It
was reasoning *plus* right feeling ; but no
divine testimony at all.

Still Dr. N. says that did not satisfy
him. " It was beautiful and religious, but
it did not even profess to be logical."
" My argument is in outline as follows :
That that absolute certitude which we were
able to possess, whether as to truths of
natural theology, or as to the fact of a
revelation, was the result of an *assemblage*
of concurring and converging probabilities,
and that, both according to the constitution of the human mind and the will of
its Maker ; that certitude was a habit
of mind, that certainty was a quality
of propositions," and so forth. (p. 20.)

There are degrees, consequently, creating certitude, opinion, etc.

Now it is quite certain that there is no divine ground of faith at all here, no testimony of God received as such; and if I take these probabilities as that on which the reception of a testimony is based, the certainty of that testimony cannot be beyond the certainty that it is a true one. Nothing can be clearer than that, whatever he might have had in his soul for the foundation of all his inquiry, no ground of divine faith existed at all. He was already on the ground of Romanism on this point—that is, of infidelity. Such a process of reasoning may show the folly of infidel reasoning, and so far be useful as a means; it never can give divine faith; it is not on the ground of it at all.

I might multiply quotations; I only add a few, to show he was always on this ground. Thus, he preached against the danger of being swayed by our feeling rather than our reason in religious enquiry. "I wish to go by reason, not by feeling." This was in 1843–4, on the eve of his becoming a Romanist: "I say that I believed in God on a ground of probability, that I believed in Christianity on a probability, and that I believed in Catholicism on a probability," and that all three were about the same kind of probabilities, "a cumulative, a transcendent probability, but still probability; inasmuch as He who made us has so willed, that in mathematics indeed we should arrive at certitude by rigid demonstration, but in religious enquiry we should arrive at certitude by accumulated probabilities." He has willed that we should so act, and co-operates with us in our acting, and therefore bestows on us "a certitude which rises higher than the logical force of our conclusions." (p. 199.) Thus we have God's grace helping us in ascertaining probabilities; but, as Dr. N. says, still probability. Now it is perfectly certain that there is no divine ground of faith here at all. No true believer, no one who has received God's testimony, and set to his seal that God is true, be he Roman Catholic itself, but knows this has nothing whatever to do with divine faith. It would be a blasphemy to talk of God's testimony being probably true, no matter how high the probability may go. Probability of conclusions is not of the same nature as reception of a testimony.

I might here again add quotations, but they are useless after these. The Romanism of Dr. Newman is not divine faith at all.

I shall now show further that the principles which led him to the place where he is were all derived from man. This may be very clever with a view to involve Anglicanism in his present position,

but is a distinct testimony that all was
built on human influences, not on God's
word or truth divinely received in any
way. Dr. Hawkins gave him Sumner
on apostolic preaching. Thus he gave
up his remaining Calvinism, and received
the doctrine of baptismal regeneration.
Another principle he received from Dr.
Hawkins was the doctrine of tradition :
" To learn doctrine we must have recourse
. . . to the catechisms and creeds . . .
after learning from them the doctrines
of Christianity, the inquirer must verify
them from scripture." (p. 9.)   Let me say
here, I distinguish fully between learning
truth and a standard of it ; but this is a
poor teaching. The first Christians certainly did not learn it from creeds or
catechism, for there were none to learn
them from ; and now a parent, as well
as a catechism, a friend, a minister, may
have taught us the truth, or Scripture
may have done so. Scripture is the *only*

standard. The fallacy of the statement is in this, that catechisms and creeds are here introduced, not as teaching, but as authority; that is, the Church is. We have received the truth from them, as truth, without saying so. Let it be true or false, it is a deceitful presentation of the matter. A parent, a friend, a minister, are not an authority. If catechisms and creeds are only means of learning, there are a hundred others. Their authority is at the root of this tradition.

But to proceed : " The Rev. Wm. James taught me the doctrine of apostolic succession." (p. 10.) "About this date . . . I read Bishop Butler's Analogy; the study of which has been to so many, as it was to me, an era in their religious opinions." (p. 10.) From him he learned the doctrine of probability. He had thus given up his early religious convictions, imbibed with what converted him to God, and was prepared for his departure into Romanism. He had been taught by man, and was landed in the denial of divine faith, on the ground of probability as the basis of religious views. Whately then taught him to think and use his reason, "to see with my own eyes, and to walk with my own feet." (p. 11.) He learnt from him "the existence of the Church as a substantive body or corporation. This led, in its effects, to Tractarianism." (p. 12.) Keble's poetry, that is, the sacramental system, subsequently exercised a great influence over him, and what was added to the doctrine of probability, of which we have spoken. (p. 17.) Froude, a hard rider, we are told, on horseback and in views, professed openly his admiration of the Church of Rome, and his hatred of the reformers. His opinions arrested and influenced Dr. N.; he was his bosom friend. (pp. 23, 24.) Mr. Froude was evidently governed by the wild imagination of an unhealthy

mind and a strong will. The theory of
virginity, and the real presence, and
mediæval antiquity, carried him away—
not the primitive Church. He went
abroad ill, and was shocked by the degeneracy which, says Dr. Newman, *he thought*
he saw in the Catholics of Italy. He died
young. "There is one remaining *source
of my opinions*," says Dr. N. (so little
conscious is he of what that means, the
tale it tells), "to be mentioned." (p. 25.)
This was the study of Fathers and Church
history, which resulted in his work as to
the Arians of the fourth century. He
delighted in and received Clement of
Alexandria's wild views. They came like
music to his inward ear, reviving the self-
invented Berkleyanism he was in when
young, of which we will speak further on.
From this school he learnt what he held
about angels. As wild as need be. He
then went abroad ill with Mr. Froude,
visited Italy and Sicily, and (with a strong

impression he was called to some work, of which anon) he began the *Tracts for the Times.*

I have gone through the proofs that God's truth was not what Dr. Newman sought, but to settle the question between the principles of Catholicity and Antiquity, or Romanism and Anglicanism ; that men's opinions, not God's word, was what gradually led him on, and that he had no divine foundation for faith at all, but avowedly only probability, which in its nature excludes the idea of the reception of a divine testimony.   I will now enquire a little into his actual progress, in which, it seems to me, astonishing levity of mind is exhibited, a large share of self-confidence, it may be some more direct power of the enemy. I shall be forgiven (as instructively tracing the elements of a history, given to us by himself, which has taken the course Dr. Newman's has) in remarking how much he was occupied with himself.   At page 3 he records the phases of his youthful feeling; he kept even his Latin verses and copy books, made and used when a young boy. Small things, but which show the tone and character of mind which were fully developed in after life, as here depicted. When he left his tutorship for the continent, he had a vision of some future before him, and on his return felt he had a work to do. "I was naturally led to think that some inward changes, as well as some larger course of action, was coming upon me." (p. 32.) His imagination was wild and unrestrained, too, and somehow or other formed in a popish school. He headed his first copy book as a child with a crucifix and rosary, and crossed himself before going into the dark, before he was fifteen; longed that the Arabian tales should be true; thought life might be a dream, or himself an angel; the world a deception, and his fellow-angels concealing themselves from him,

F

and deceiving him with the semblance of a material world. (p. 2.)

Nor when a clergyman had this character disappeared.   In 1834 he said of the angels in a sermon, " Every breath of air, and ray of light and heat, every beautiful prospect, is as it were the skirts of their garments, the waving of the robes of those whose faces see God." (p. 28.)   "Again I ask, What would be the thoughts of a man who, examining a flower, or an herb, or a pebble, or a ray of light, which he treats as something so beneath him in the scale of existence, suddenly discovered that he was in the presence of some powerful being,, who was hidden behind the visible things he was inspecting, who, &c. . . . nay, whose robe and ornament these objects were?" (p. 28.)   "Also, besides the hosts of evil spirits, I considered there was a middle race, δαιμόνια, neither in heaven nor in hell; partially fallen, capricious, wayward; noble or crafty, benevolent or malicious, as the case might be. These beings gave a sort of inspiration or intelligence to races, nations, and classes of men. Hence the action of bodies politic," &c. (p. 29.) This is connected with his study of Clemens Alexandrinus and Alexandrianism, that is, of the Neoplatonism which corrupted the gospel, and was the true source of Arianism. This Clemens himself being unsound, and Justin Martyr expressly declaring that it was impossible the supreme God could be made flesh.

However, my present object is to show the kind of preparation there was in the state of his mind for his further progress. Depth of conscience, sense of good and evil, the soberness of God's word, subjection to it, one finds no trace of. It is superficial imagination, and, on such subjects, levity. And he pursued this out. " I cannot but think that there are beings with a great deal of good in them, yet with great defects, who are the animating principles of certain institutions, &c., &c. Take England, with many high virtues and yet a low Catholicism." (p. 29.) This is in 1837. In 1835–6 he had before him the whole state of the question between Anglicanism and Romanism (p. 111), so that these wild wanderings of mind existed and entered into his judgment of England's ecclesiastical state. Is there anything of earnestness or an exercised conscience here?

I have said there was self-confidence and levity in dealing with solemn subjects. What I mean now by the latter is this. When he was uncertain what he believed, what was the truth, and where it would lead, though growingly inclined to Romanism, he went on acting diligently on the minds of others. He was not at rest himself (he tells us so), yet went on influencing others ; not always saying all he had in his mind, but enough to prepare theirs for it. Now, on so solemn a subject as what is the true religion, to act week after

week on others without knowing oneself
what is that true religion, I call moral
levity of the worst kind. That he was
not at rest, he tells us. (p. 119.) "And first
I will say, whatever comes of saying it
(for I leave inferences to others), that for
years I must have had something of an
habitual notion, though it was latent, and
had never led me to distrust my own convictions, that my mind had not found its
ultimate rest, and that in some sense or
other I was on journey." This was the
case as early as 1833, and even 1829.
Now, what does this show? That with
the consciousness of changing views, his
mind on a journey he knew not whither,
he went on leading and directing others,
by sermons, tracts, &c. Now, I do think
an earnest, serious, conscientious man
would not have done this; a modest man
would not, he would have waited till he
saw what the truth was himself, till he was
at the end of his journey. And why did

he go on when he knew he had not come to any settled conclusion? Because he had immense confidence in himself. He never was led to distrust his own convictions (that is, himself—his own mind), though they were changing every day; he was on his "journey." This is what I call moral levity and self-confidence.

But we may have some other elements of this. The truth is, that at this moment all was over as to Anglicanism in Dr. N.'s mind. It was in a ruinous, evil state; he could and was to reform it. But we have the sources of this movement in his mind; it was in full connection with angelical flowers and pebbles. It was not an earnest inquiry into what Paul taught, or John presses on us in the power of the eternal Spirit—not a heart bowed by Christ's words, and because the Church does not answer to what she ought to be for her heavenly Bridegroom. It was not the truth, it was not God's word, it was not what God planted at the first wholly a right seed (to make use of Jeremiah's expression as to Israel), nothing of the moral depth of the exercised conscience which such thoughts are connected with, of which heart-connection with Christ, and the desire that the church might be what it ought to be for Him, as the word of God will show it to us, are the source of in the heart. It was Alexandria. So Dr. N. tells.

He had been writing the history of the Arians. He had found in the wild mysteries and errors of Platonistic Christianity "the primeval mystery,"* that all nature was a

---

* I should have doubted what Dr. N. meant by the primeval mystery, but for the words "to which I had so great a devotion in my youth." This was the Platonic system of ideas and demons, material things being merely a representative to sense of archetypal truth. This, though Neoplatonism properly speaking, was a subsequent system, a last effort of philosophy against Christianity, reigned among the Alexandrian fathers. Justin Martyr never gave up his philosopher's cloak. Clement had his common teaching, and his esoteric for the initiated.

parable, the world the expression of the Λόγος, or word of God, the stars living beings. For such was Alexandrian philosophy, as displayed in Philo,* and with which the Alexandrian fathers were more

* That all this doctrine about souls and angels, or demons, is half Platonic, half philosopho-Mosaic, is unquestionable. It had a semi-Jewish, semi-heathen origin, coming, I doubt not, as no one who has examined Manicheism, Gnosticism, and Eastern or old Persian views, can, I think, question, from the East. Philo represents the mixture in the Lord and apostles' time. He held that all was full of living beings (the sun, moon, and stars being not only animals, but most pure minds); that all the air, the space from the moon, the extreme of heaven proper, to the earth, was filled with souls as numerous as the stars; that the higher ones were very pure, and were demons, called angels by Moses, the lower ones loved getting down into human bodies; the root of all the doctrine being the evil of matter. See Philo περὶ Γεν. (i. 263 Mangey) περὶ Φυτ. Νωε (i. 331), περὶ τε θεοπ. ον. (i. 641), and elsewhere. This Origen held to be true. He maintains it largely : De Prin. lib. i. 7. (i. 72, 73, De la Rue), and that they first had a body, and that then a soul entered into it, which desires to depart and be with Christ. Clement is said to have denied it. I cannot find the passage. In the system referred to above, these demons, or angels, were held to be intercessors, as the Jews also taught.

or less imbued. "In her triumphant zeal in behalf of that primeval mystery, to which I had so great a devotion from my youth, I recognised the movement of my Spiritual Mother. '*Incessu patuit Dea.*' The self-conquest of her Ascetics, the patience of her Martyrs, the irresistible determination of her Bishops, the joyous swing of her advance, both exalted and abashed me. I said to myself, 'Look on this picture and on that' (the Anglican Church). I felt affection for my own Church, but not tenderness; I felt dismay at her prospects, anger and scorn at her do-nothing perplexity. . . . I saw that Reformation principles were powerless to rescue her. As to leaving her, the thought never crossed my imagination; still, I ever kept before me that there was something greater than the Established Church, and that was the Church Catholic and Apostolic set up from the beginning, of which she was but the local presence and organ.

She was nothing unless she was this. She must be dealt with strongly, or she would be lost. There was need of a second reformation." (p. 32.) Now, although Dr. N. speaks of the Primitive Church, he refers essentially to Alexandria. He says (p. 26), "What principally attached me to the ante-Nicene period was the great Church of Alexandria, the historical centre of teaching of those times." "The broad philosophy of Clement and Origen carried me away." And this is distinctly connected with his rhapsodies about angels, &c. It is the whole subject from page 25 to page 32. This was what he admired; this forced reformation on his notice. He owed his doctrine about angels to the Alexandrian school. He was "drifted back first to the ante-Nicene history, and then to the Church of Alexandria." (p. 26.) It was the Alexandrian Church led him to his reforming undertakings.

Let us see a little what the state of this

Church was, and in matters which made Dr. N. admire it and seek to reform the Anglican. Strange to say, it is, to say the very least, excessively doubtful whether for years, yea centuries, there was any episcopal ordination there at all, at least if we are to believe St. Jerome. No doubt in his time, and before it, episcopacy was established, and this he recognizes. But on the pretensions of the diaconate at Rome, he exalts presbyters, declaring that according to scripture bishops and presbyters were identical; he says the apostle perspicuously teaches that presbyters are the same as bishops; quotes Phil. i., Acts xx. 28, Titus i. 5 *seq.*, 1 Tim. iv. 14, 1 Peter v., and the 2nd and 3rd epistles of John. But he adds, that afterwards one was chosen who should be set over the others, as a remedy for schism, lest any drawing to himself should make a breach in the Church of Christ. For at Alexandria also, from the evangelist Mark up to the bishops

Heraclas and Dionysius, the presbyters always called bishop one chosen out of themselves, placed in a higher grade ; as if the army should make an Imperator (as they did in the empire), or the deacons choose from themselves one whom they may have known to be industrious, and called him Archdeacon. Now it is true, he adds, that the bishop differs only in this, that he can ordain. Nor do I doubt for a moment, that was the universal order in Jerome's time. Nay, the Alexandrian patriarch, whose jurisdiction then was larger than that of Rome, claimed the right to ordain in all his subject-dioceses himself. But it is equally true that Jerome states historically that it had not been so till Heraclas and Dionysius ; and this is confirmed by many peculiarities as to the rights of Alexandrian presbyters, and, as is said, the abolition of their rights by Alexander in the time of the Nicene council. But this by-the-bye.

That Alexandrian theology was philosophical, and corrupted by philosophy, is certain; Clement, the great Alexandrian teacher does not conceal it. He says in his Stromata (ed. Potter i. p. 319, line 35), speaking of the nourishment of souls, the peace in the word, and the life which is of God, he adds: " For souls have their own nourishment, some growing in knowledge and intelligence, some fed according to the Grecian philosophy, of which, as in the case of nuts, all is not edible." In lib. vii. 2 (p. 831, 2), "the Word teaches all, some as friends, some as faithful servants, some as servants; he is the teacher who instructs the man of knowledge (the Gnostic) in mysteries (this is the esoteric teaching for a few), the faithful by good hopes, and the hard-hearted by corrective discipline and sensible (esthetic) powers." And afterwards: " He, the Word, it is who gives philosophy to the Greeks by inferior angels; for the angels, by a divine and ancient ordinance, are distributed by nations, but the doctrine of believers is the Lord's part, insisting on the divine care of all." So in book vi. 8 (p. 773). "All things useful to life are given by the Word, but philosophy more especially to the Greeks was given to them as a special covenant, to be as a foundation of philosophy according to Christ." And in book i. 6 (p. 337) he makes the sower of the parable to have come thus from above from the foundation of the world. What this philosophy was he tells us (p. 338): "Philosophy, I say not the Stoic, not the Platonic, nor the Epicurean and Aristotelic, but whatever things are said rightly by each of these sects, teaching righteousness with pious intelligence; this, as a whole, I call eclectic philosophy." The law, he says elsewhere, was for the Jews, philosophy for the Greeks, till Christ came (vi. 17, p. 823); the whole chapter being a long discourse on this subject, each receiving it according to their deserts.

I am fully satisfied that the East was the origin of much more of all this than we are aware of, corrected partially in these Alexandrian fathers by Christianity, and already in Plato (and, I suppose, Pythagoras) by Grecian habits of thought. The root of it was, that there was a supreme unknown God who dwelt in the depths of silence, and could have no connection with matter. Hence emanations and the Demiurge, an inferior creator, resulting in Gnosticism—the plague of the early Church. Platonism, with its emanated demons, and the Alexandrian philosophy, divides into the Christian and heathen parties, Clement giving his perfect Christian the name of Gnostic. Early there was a Jewish party, whom Philo represents. In all, Logos was an inferior being, though divine. It resulted, in another form, in Arianism, the doctrine more or less of the Alexandrian ante-Nicene Fathers (not of Irenæus), combated by Athanasius when it came formally to a head in Arius. Thus it was that Dr. Newman came to be called an Arian. He had imbibed a delight in these ante-Nicene statements. Hence, too, arose asceticism. Matter held, as Plato teaches, the soul down as a nail to earth; it was to be mortified. Asceticism began in the Alexandrian Church, partly indeed by persons who fled in the Decian persecution. Hence forbidding to marry, not that people might be more devoted, but as evil for the Gnostic.

Again, Origen—a most attractive, interesting man, I fully admit, but whose name became the football of passion in the Church—what was he? First he applied to himself literally by mutilation Matthew xix. 12. He held that souls were born into different conditions in this world, according to their conduct in a previously existing state—a doctrine current among the heathen Egyptians, but a well known eastern idea of Buddhists and Brahmins too. Buddha's great doctrine was, how to escape it by hearing "Bana," and absolute indifference to everything sense could feel, so as to obtain Nirwana (extinction). But Origen held—it is not my part to make him consistent—that the fall (and this was Alexandrian and Philo's doctrine already, and Platonic) was the pure soul of man coming into a body. He was not sound, though he seems sometimes to be clear, on the divinity of Christ. As to the divinity of the Holy Ghost, he was wholly unsound. As to Ammonius (the master of Heraclas the Patriarch, and others), it is disputed whether he is Christian or heathen.

Such was the school Dr. N. delighted in—their philosophy, he tells us, not their theology ; but it is impossible to separate them. The fall of man being a pure soul coming into material body—is that philosophy or theology ? Even as to Christ (*Origen de Principiis*, book ii., c. 6 ; *De*

G

Incarnatione, i. 90, ed. De la Rue), holding, as he does expressly, that the divine nature cannot, without a mediator, be united to a body, and each soul receiving according to its deserts, he states that the Word or Son took one of these previously existing souls from the beginning of creation, and became and remained thoroughly one spirit with him; and then, by the mediation of that, took a body too, though he admits it is beyond even the apostle's thoughts.* I need not go further.   Men's souls were to work their way back to liberation from matter—as also Philo and their Platonic predecessors and Gnostic contemporaries held—that was the object of the mission of Christ.

To prove the effect of this heathenish system in morals, I may add—what I regret to have to add, but with modern pretensions in these things it is well it

* He applies John x. 18 to the inseparability of the soul and the Word.

should be known — that one form of
asceticism was the clergy abstaining from
marriage, under the plea of purity, taking
to sleep with them women with the same
pretension to purity, alleging they were
free from all evil of mind. This was one
form of asceticism—not the only one. I
know they went into the desert. But this
shows the nature of it. This Dr. N.
must know as well as possible. He will
say it was often publicly condemned. It
was often condemned in the East and in
the West, but that shows it was a custom ;
and they had a name, both in Greek
and Latin — Συνεισακταί (*subintroductæ*),
and ἀγαπηταί (beloved). Irenæus himself
charges the Gnostics with the same
practice. It is recognised in the Shepherd
of Hermas (III. sim. ix. 11), which was
read in the churches—there, of course,
in a seemly way. Tertullian, when a
Montanist, charges the Catholics with it.
(*De Jejuniis*, p. 554.) My reader will

easily understand that it is not only in
reference to Dr. Newman I quote these
things : we learn what early infected the
Church. But we do see the wild system
which attracted Dr. N., and sanctioned
his early mental vagaries, preached to his
parishioners, be it remembered, at St.
Mary's.

After this Dr. N. went abroad. Here
it was he had the strong impression that
he was called to reform Anglicanism.
Let us retrace his history thus far. He
was converted, he tells us, at fifteen. He
believed, too, that the inward conversion
of which he was conscious (and of which
he still is more certain than that he has
hands and feet) would last into the next
life, and that he was elected to eternal
glory. (p. 4.) This was a beginning of
divine faith, a great change of thoughts.
The influence and books, he tells us, were
of the Calvinistic school. He, humanly
speaking, almost owed his soul to one

good man, whom he does not name. But all the special truth which wrought this in 1822, save the fact of heaven and hell, divine favour and divine wrath, of the justified and unjustified, which alone took root in his mind, did not remain with him many years. In 1832 he came under very different influences. On reading Sumner he gave up all his remaining Calvinism. He never believed in reprobation. From Dr. Hawkins he received the doctrine of tradition; from the Rev. W. James, apostolic succession; from Butler's Analogy he learnt to rest his faith in probability,* not on divine testimony; from Whately, to think and use his reason, and see with his own eyes,

* It is a singular effect of this reasoning on probability, and I must add of the Aristotelian teaching of Oxford, that in this famous and able book to which Dr. N. refers (Butler's Analogy), it is stated, that the natural propensities of man must continue in heaven, as happiness cannot be without virtue, nor virtue without trial and exercise. Such is the fruit of ignorance of redemption.

and believe in the existence of the Church as a proper corporate body; Keble added faith and love in man to probability, to give it force, leading him to authority; Froude led him in his feelings towards Rome, and hatred of the reformers. (pp. 5–25.) This brought him to Alexandria, or at least co-operated with it; for the dates mingle together at the close of this history. There we have now found him, and going abroad to rest himself after his labours in this ante-Nicene study, his wild Platonism in full blow.

There was need of a second reformation. Who was to do it? Here comes the turning point in Dr. N.'s life. I do not doubt the direct agency of Satan on a self-

Bishop Butler's words are these: "This way of putting the matter supposes particular affections" (or propensions, as he calls them) "to remain in a future state, which it is scarce possible to avoid supposing." And he is speaking of "the danger finite creatures are in from the very nature of propensions or particular affections." (Part I. chap. v., on "Moral Discipline.")

confident mind ; but I must trace it in its
human manifestation. " Exchanging as I
was definite tutorial work . . . . for
foreign countries and an unknown future.
I naturally was led to think that some
inward changes, as well as some larger
course of action, were coming upon me."
(p. 32). At this moment, while waiting
at Whitchurch for the mail, he wrote the
verses about his guardian angel—

"Are these the tracks of some unearthly friend?"

and goes on to speak of the "vision that
haunted him." (p. 32.) Why, when jaded
with study, and obliged to go abroad for
his health, was it natural to look for some
larger course of action ? There is a
natural, though unconfessed, sentiment of
force in every active mind ; but in the
Christian, suppressed by the sense of his
own nothingness, that without Christ he
can do nothing, and the principle of obedience, than which nothing is more humble,

and of conscience, which makes our own
path being right of the first importance.
Dr. N. had this confidence; he thought of
acting on others—a larger course of action.
I quite believe he was afterwards unaware
of the influence he exercised on young
men; that is very often the case.

But the sick man, filled with his primeval mystery, and inclined towards Rome,
having left all the forms of truth that had
been the means of his conversion, was
looking for a second reformation, and,
through a "vision," a larger course of
action for himself.   His journey completes
this picture.   He was not much amongst
Roman Catholics.   His imagination was
at work on new scenes naturally enough.
"The sight of so many great places,
venerable shrines, and noble churches,
much impressed my imagination," he tells
us.   He heard singing in a country church
at six o'clock, and his heart thus also was
touched. (p. 53.)   Now, a religious congre-

gation singing, when heard from without, has this effect—touches deeply the religious imagination where it exists. It could not have been anything really spiritual in his mind; for he did not know what they were singing. In his weary days at Palermo, "I was not ungrateful for the comfort which I had received in frequenting the churches, nor did I ever forget it." Then, again, "her zealous maintenance of the doctrine and rule of celibacy, which I recognized as apostolic, and her faithful agreement with Antiquity in so many other points which were dear to me, was an argument, as well as a plea, in favour of the great Church of Rome. Thus I learned to have tender feelings towards her; but still my reason was not affected at all." (p. 54.)

Now you will remark, as I said at the beginning, all is sensuous here, what acts on the imagination; no question of truth and grace, no holiness, unless celibacy be

taken for it, which he believed apostolic—
not, observe, self-devotedness, when given
of God, which is apostolic, but as a rule;
which is so false, that it shows Dr. N. was
wholly governed by imagination. Not
only does the apostle say, the elder is to
be the husband of one wife, having his
children subject in all gravity, and let us
know that Peter and the Lord's brethren
were married, though he and Barnabas
were not; but in the council of Nice,
which Dr. N. had been just studying, it
was formally refused to be made a rule,
though it had acquired great influence,
and was resisted by Paphnutius, an unmarried bishop, as a snare. What its
enforcement in the eleventh century, by
Hildebrand (though never carried through
till the end of the thirteenth), produced,
is well known. I may speak of it further
on, when I come to speak of the causes
of Protestantism. A man must have
been wholly blinded by imagination, or

Satan, to say celibacy was, as a rule, apostolic. Even the Roman body holds it for a mere matter of discipline; the Greek requires that priests should be married—only bishops not, if I do not mistake.

His imagination was fully ripened towards Rome; the primitive Church, that is, not the Scripture, or first, but the ante-Nicene Church* was certainly right, the Anglican useless if it was not the same; he was tenderly turned towards Rome, as to his heart, and, at any rate, Anglicanism needed a second reformation; he had no tenderness, he tells us, for it. Rome was a great Church, his heart with her; his habits, no doubt, not overcome, he might hope to defend Anglicanism, but it was dreadfully bad. The whole was a foregone conclusion. What was the work he was going to

* We have no accounts, I may say, of the Church from apostolic men to Justin Martyr.

do? He had entire, thorough confidence in himself—confidence unrepressed by grace. The motto chosen from Homer by Froude, showing his own feeling, he adds, too, shows this transparently, "You shall know the difference now that I am back again." Nor does he conceal from himself what I am proving—"I began to think I had a mission." (p. 34.) Nor was it an uncertainty. He visited Monsignore Wiseman. He wished they should visit Rome a second time. He saw plain enough his state, as he did afterwards what was going on at Oxford. (p. 64.) Dr. N. replied to him, with great gravity, "We have a work to do in England;" pleased to pander to Romanism, and be in Monsignore's good graces. The state of his mind was shown; when sick, he cried, "I shall not die, I shall not die, for I have not sinned against light." (p. 35.) No peaceful conscience, no rest in Christ;

the latent conviction he speaks of, of
not being at rest, ceased to be latent
when death seemed to be there. The
pressure of darkness on a troubled conscience, used, I doubt not, by the enemy;
but still, conscience, which, if not settled
between him and God, Satan would drive
him to quiet in his own way. He was
sobbing bitterly, while waiting to leave
Palermo, and replied, to the inquiry of
his servant, "I have a work to do in
England."

Now this uneasiness, if not a bad
conscience in a general way, of which,
of course, I can say nothing, and is not
here so presented, was a bad conscience,
which, not possessing Christ for its own
rest in Him, looked to the Church,
because it had not rest; and from his
previous studies, feeling he did not
possess that, and had resisted im-
pressions and feelings which led him
to Romanism, broke out in bitter un-

easiness when thus ill.   But remark, no
destruction of self-confidence, no turning
to Christ in lowliness of conscience and
heart.   He turned to self.   " I could
only answer, I have a work to do."
This work he was doing afterwards.
The rest was merely a process, a question
of time.   He hated Protestantism, he
loved Popery, though not agreeing with it.
Anglicanism was all wrong, even if it
were on the foundation.   He pretended
to set about and correct it.   Romanism
was the only certainly right thing in
existence.   The primitive Church had
been right and lovely—the only right
thing now was Romanism; he hoped to
get Anglicanism on right ground, but he
had no tenderness for her.   And now it
is I find the excessive moral levity of
Dr. Newman's state, of which I have
spoken, come out in full blaze.   It was
no search for the truth, as such, for
himself; he had not accepted all Rome's

doctrines, but neither had he when he joined her; but she was the only right Church in his eyes: he was looking for the church of his imagination, not for truth.* He did not believe transubstantiation the day he joined Popery, more than twenty years before. He says so. After joining Rome as infallible, he accepted it on authority.

See what a state this involves. There were two real religions: Protestantism and Popery. The former he hated. Seeking communion with Protestants was the last blow to Anglicanism. (p. 142.) He counted them heretics. Rome, when abroad, he held as undeniably the most exalted church in the whole world, mani-festing, in all the truth and beauty of the Spirit, high-mindedness, majesty, and the calm consciousness of power. Anglican-

* I say, the Church of his imagination; he says, Popery is a religion—Protestantism is a religion; the *via media* is only on paper. (p. 68.)

ism, bishops and all, was at best as a set of unruly boys—Trojans, who would know the difference when he came back. Hence, afterwards, when they trench on his *via media*, he threatens them all. There was a limit to forbearance. Anglicanism still remained to be tried. He looked to "that future of the Anglican Church which was to be a new birth of the ancient religion"; a system which would be rising up. (p. 101.)

Thus inclined to Rome, hating Protestantism, Anglicanism being nothing really, he set about to work. Did he ascertain the truth before he set to work? In no wise. I do not mean that he did not like the ante-Nicene Church. No doubt he did. But had he searched out the grounds of truth, or truth itself, before he acted? In no wise. Antiquity was his only ground. "Taking *Antiquity*," he says, referring back to this early period, "not the *Existing Church*, as the oracle of truth." (p. 156.) Never, mark, the Word. "I thought that the Church of England was substantially founded upon them" [the Fathers.] (p. 56.) Had he searched them thoroughly? Not at all. "I did not know all that the Fathers had said, but I felt that, even when their tenets happened to differ from the Anglican, no harm could come of reporting them. I said out what I was clear they had said; I spoke vaguely and imperfectly of what I thought they had said, or what some of them had said. Anyhow, no harm could come of bending the crooked stick the other way, in the process of straightening it; it was impossible to break it." (p. 56.) Thus Anglicanism was but a stick to be straightened. He set about reforming, rebuilding the Church, getting a Church *de facto* of flesh and bones, as he says—held the Fathers to be the authority, yet did not know all that they had said. Can there be con-

ceived, on so solemn a subject, a man
acting with more self - confidence and
more levity? Nor does he deny it. "I
never had the staidness or dignity necessary for a leader." "I had a lounging,
free and easy way of carrying things on."
(p. 59.) Now this is true; but think of a
man saying it of his whole status as to
the Church of God, and in the things in
which he was acting as one who had a
mission to reform the Church, and rebuild
it in its beauty as of old.

He admits (pp. 58, 59) he was widely
spreading his principles, not recognizing
the hold he had over young men. He
laughed when a man innocently thought
he meant "sacrament" when he said the
"sacrifice" of the Eucharist, and did not
give himself the trouble of answering it.
Accordingly, he tells us, when Dr. Pusey
joined the movement, he (Dr. P.) saw
that there ought to be more sobriety, more
gravity, more careful pains, more sense of

responsibility in the Tracts and in the whole movement. It was through him the character of the Tracts was changed. (p. 62.) He, however grieved, and, as I judge, justly, though I may not agree with all his views;* and Mr. Keble, in the sense of that responsibility, have as yet remained in Anglicanism.

And that he acted in this lounging, easy way, was so truly the case, that while quite settled in what he was seeking to establish—"a visible Church with sacraments and rites which are the channels of invisible grace"—yet he tells us that he did not know what he aimed at. "I thought that this was the doctrine of Scripture, of the early Church, and of the Anglican Church." Of this he never ceased to be certain; but "in 1834 and

---

* I think the whole Catholic system, Roman or Anglican, wrong in confounding "the body" of Ephesians i. with "the house" of Ephesians ii., and attributing to the house now the privileges of the body.

the following years I put this ecclesiastical doctrine on a broader basis after reading Laud, Bramhall, Stillingfleet, and other Anglican divines on the one hand, and after prosecuting the study of the Fathers on the other." (p. 49.)

Now, that he held a doctrine immaturely no one can blame; we have all done so. But that he should set about to reform and rebuild the Church with a special mission, though he founded it on the Fathers, with his views unformed, seems to me, I confess, intolerable self-sufficiency and levity. "When I began the *Tracts for the Times*, I rested the main doctrine, of which I am speaking, upon Scripture, and on the Anglican Prayer Book, and on St. Ignatius' epistles." (p. 50.) The visible Church on Scripture, sacraments and sacramental rites on the Prayer Book, the Episcopal system on St. Ignatius. Now the Scripture clearly teaches a visible Church, and thus is authority that there ought to be one. As to the fact, it is all around us. But why not search Scripture as to what it ought to be? I believe it is sadly fallen; but why not go to Paul, and John, and Peter, to know what it ought to be, instead of Ignatius? And note the excessive inconsistency after all: he is going to build a right Church, because Anglicanism was not such; and yet he takes the Prayer Book of Anglicans as the rule to prove his point on the matter he was anxious about, although he admits "that the Anglican Church must have a ceremonial, a ritual, and a fulness of doctrine and devotion which it had not at present"! (p. 166.) Was this because it was right? No; "if it were to compete with the Roman Church with any prospect of success." Why so? Because he liked that system, not because it could be any authority for truth; for the system he was seeking to change. It suited him, the Articles did not. And they were to be interpreted according to Catholic teaching, not the opinion of the framers. "Catholicism" (by which he then meant Romanism), he tells us plainly later, "was the real scope and issue of the movement." And why does he take Ignatius? Why do all, who love the system Dr. N. has followed? Why did I myself delight in it, found my thoughts on him? Because he already liked and had adopted the system found in his published writings, not from any real, ascertained authority in Ignatius.

Dr. N. must have well known, that since Ussher and Daillé they have been called in question; that there are two recensions, besides confessedly spurious letters, one enormously interpolated, the other shorter; so that, though defended by learned men, as a document they were of questionable authority. Since then it has been, I think I may say, ascertained —I do not say all acquiesce in it—that

five out of the eight letters are wholly
spurious, and the three remaining ones,
even in the short recension, interpolated,
and the passages in favour of unity which
Dr. N. delighted in, are all, save one, false
and spurious; for you must know that
these pious frauds were the custom of this
vaunted primitive church.   There was one
Leucas, or Lucius, who had quite a manu-
factory of them.   I do not know that it
was he who tampered with Ignatius.
There were numbers of false Gospels *
and Acts of the apostles, and that not
only by heretics, but by pious people, and
this very early indeed.

Dr. Newman scarcely even excuses
himself here; if he does, it is only for
guilt in his vain confidence, so far as he
had strong persuasions in 1832, which he
has since given up.   I do not blame him

---

* A pretty copious list of these pious frauds, so-called,
is in Baronius, i. 302. The Gospels have been collected
by Fabricius and Theile.

for giving up what he thought wrong. I blame him for lightly pretending to reform and rebuild the Anglican body, that is, to form a church as it should be, when he had not searched the grounds on which he did it; when he knew he was not at rest, but on journey, as he has told us, and doing it in a free and easy way, and, I must say, with some effrontery, telling us that he " had a lounging, free and easy way " in the matter. Was this God-fearing? The more his book is read through, the more it will be seen. Yet he attaches immense importance to his movement. He says, with singular self-complacency, " Great acts take time. At least, this is what I felt in my own case." (p. 169.) He sought, he tells us elsewhere, to go by reason, not sentiment; here, that " all the logic in the world would not have made him move faster." God does not save people by logic. This when people showed him the evident and necessary consequences of his principles. More of this when his pleas as to his honesty are considered. I do not suppose he was a concealed Roman Catholic before he professed to be so, in the least; but he did know long before where all was tending, and knew he was leading others there, and continued to do so while unsettled, and, full of confidence in himself, charged others as authors of it for resisting him. Yet it did lead him there.

But what I insist on now is, the moral levity of teaching without his mind having arrived at any conclusions. He says, " Alas! it was my portion for whole years to remain, without any satisfactory basis for my religious profession, in a state of moral sickness, neither able to acquiesce in Anglicanism, nor able to go to Rome." (p. 66.) Now these are the very years in which he was labouring as having a special mission, influencing diligently others, taking the future of Anglicanism and of souls on

his own shoulders.   He had confidence
in his cause, despised every rival system
of doctrine, had a thorough contempt
for the evangelical system.   Owing to
this confidence, there was a mixture of
fierceness and sport in his behaviour.   If he
had brought men on to a certain point, if
they stopped he did not care ; he liked to
make them preach the truth without knowing it, and encouraged them so to do.   " I
was not unwilling to draw an opponent
on step by step by virtue of his own
opinions to the brink of some intellectual
absurdity, and to leave him to get back
as he could." (p. 45.)   He speaks of the
imprudence and wantonness into which
his absolute confidence in his cause led
him.   I understand this state of mind in
a restless spirit confident in his views, but
which has found no rest for itself—excited
and uneasy, "moral sickness," as he admits.
But is it God-fearing ?   Is it God-fearing
to teach others and set the Church right

in such a state? Can we be surprised at the result? And what must we think of the result such a course in such a state of mind led to? He tells us, that through the storm on Tract 90, he had already before lost full confidence in himself. He had confidence in the apostolic movement; "but how was I any more to have absolute confidence in myself?" (p. 89.) Did he cease to go on? No; the movement was out of his hands. But on his views he was obstinate, and bearded the bishops. This is clear: he *had had* absolute confidence in himself. He got completely bewildered in reading Bellarmine and the Anglican divines. This had no tendency whatever to harass and perplex him. "It was a matter which bore not on convictions, but on proofs." (p. 105.) But he had been teaching with absolute confidence in himself, without having ever really ascertained the difference, or found solid ground on it.

In 1839, the fact that Leo's judgment had settled the council of Chalcedon and the monophysite question, upset his *via media*, and showed that Rome was now on the ground of Leo in the fifth century, the Protestants on that of Eutychians and Monophysites, *i.e.* heretics.* (p. 115.) Here he owns he had the habitual notion that he was "on journey"—had not found his ultimate rest. Yet it had never led him to distrust his convictions. Before and after, he was restlessly teaching others. I feel I need not go further. The time of his activity, the time of his influence, was the time of his own "moral sickness" and unformed views.

* Dr. N. very conveniently forgets that Pope Leo, a very able man, who really founded the power of the Papacy, forbad that doctrine to be put in the creed, though he admits it, which makes Dr. N. himself now hold the Greeks to be heretics for not holding. And I may add that a general council, admitted such, forbad positively any additional articles to be added to the creed. That is what Dr. N. calls development.

I turn for a moment to Protestantism. Mr. N.'s position, on his return from abroad with a mission, was this—the Roman Church was the most exalted Church in the whole world (p. 121), certainly Catholic. Protestantism he hated; it was heretical, save in England; so that to receive a Protestant without abjuration of error was subsequently sufficient almost, if not quite, to oblige a person to leave the Establishment, and was what finally led to it. (pp. 142–146.) It shattered his faith in Anglicanism. Anglicanism rested only on paper, to be formed by himself by his mission. As it stood, was of questionable Catholicity; could be so only by interpreting her Articles as no one else in the world would. There was no motive for keeping aloof from Rome, but the pope's being Antichrist (p. 52); which for my part, however anti-Christian he may be, I do not believe. It appears Rome's being the great whore, drunk with the blood of the saints, was nothing. This he got over by its being the spirit of the city acting on the Church. (p. 121.) He was determined to clear Romanism. Transubstantiation he did not believe; but Mr. Palmer held, that all the decrees of Trent might have a Catholic sense. I recall his own excuses. But Rome's being the harlot drunk with blood, transubstantiation, purgatory, the worship of the virgin and the saints, indulgences, the repeated sacrifice of the mass as an expiation for the sins of the living and the dead, the supremacy and infallibility of the pope—none of these or other principles and dogmas of Rome was any ground for separation from it. It is astonishing how little hold truth had on his mind, how little prominence it had with him: a very peculiar phenomenon. Being disposed towards Rome is nothing uncommon or surprising; but souls are kept, often almost unconsciously, by some truth which guards them. I was, especially

by Hebrews ix. x. But truth, it is evident
(I do not say mere dogma common to
all), he never cared about. He says the
English opposition to Romanism was
caused by political motives in Henry the
eighth's time, than which nothing can be
more unfounded. He burnt people for
giving up his Six Articles, which were
essentially popish, though he would not
accept the pope's supremacy. The reformation in England was set on foot by
Edward VI., as to authority ; but by
saints, of whom Henry burned many, as
to truth.

But I shall show what brought in Protestantism, if it is to be used as a name. I
have no doubt there were many defects,
and could not but be, in the order that
was set up. The mere name is nothing.
It came from an act of German electors
at the Diet of Spires protesting against
the recess of that Diet, passed only by a
majority of votes when they had left,

which they held to be illegal. The Reformed are not called Protestants abroad. But Protestantism, used as a popular name, was the protest of the conscience, given energy to by faith, against the most horrible system of iniquity that ever withered and overwhelmed the human conscience. It was not merely negative; there was the positive assertion of common fundamental dogmas (this was the very object of the Confession of Augsburg, because this negative character was charged upon it) ; and articles were added which are rejected by Dr. Newman and his party—such as justification by faith, the two sacraments, and other anti-Romanist ones ; as the counter doctrine was also maintained in the decrees of the Council of Trent refuting formally this teaching ; and further, the authority of the Word of God maintained, of the books of which the Council of Trent has given an undeniably false list.

It was not simply the right of private judgment in the modern sense. The *direct* responsibility of each conscience to God, as contrasted with the domination of priests, was maintained, and rightly, as between man and man—not the right simply, but the obligation to judge, was maintained; but it was the public confession of positive truth which characterized Protestantism. Each local body framed its own profession of faith. The authority of the word of God was asserted. The right of every man to judge Scripture, or have his own thoughts where God has revealed His name, never entered into the thoughts of the Reformers. The right of private judgment, as often now talked of, whether by infidels, who desire it, or Romanists, who condemn it, is essentially and absolutely incompatible with the absolute authority of Scripture, which was the Protestant principle. The question was, What was to have authority—Scripture, or the clergy and tradition?   The duty to judge by Scripture was asserted, and rightly.*   It was the putting away of evil, and the teaching of positive faith, and the authority of the word of God, dogmatically and historically in this order.   It broke out, under Luther, by resisting indulgences, the profligate and shameless sale of which was destroying all morality, and even the parochial care of the priests.

I repeat, while truth was promulgated, and Luther's action the fruit of his having learnt the truth, the first spring of action was the revolt of the Christian conscience against the state of the professing Christian Church.   I shall give some account of the state of that Church, that it may

* My object is not here controversy, but Dr. Newman's book, or it is easy to show that Romanism has no sure ground of authority, which the Protestant has.   As to private judgment, it is all clap-trap.   The Romanist calls on me to judge Protestantism as much as I do him to judge Popery, and to judge that he is right.

be seen how far this revolt of conscience was well grounded.

And here I feel I am on painful, and, for any Christian, dangerous ground. It is, and ought to be, painful to rake up evil, especially in that which bears the name of Christ. There is danger of failing in that article of charity, "rejoiceth not in iniquity." I admit, I trust I feel, both the painfulness and the danger. But with the pretensions which are current, and the deceitful statements of morbid imaginations as to the holiness of the Romish body, it becomes necessary that those likely to be deceived should know the truth. Not only is "*corruptio optimi pessima corruptio*," but the corruption of Rome was in itself worse than any corruption that ever existed. I shall state from authentic sources, and Roman Catholic sources, what the state of things really was, and show how early it began. I have verified the statements in the authorities quoted except two—Mansi's "Councils" being inaccessible to me, and Nic. Clemangis' works not in my library. I have only Hardouins' "Councils," which does not reproduce the document; but there is no doubt it is authentic and correct.   I refer to the letter of Pope Alexander V., quoted further on.

Even in the apostles' days Paul complains that all seek their own, not the things of Jesus Christ; Jude, that evil men had crept in unawares, turning the grace of God into lasciviousness.   But then there was apostolic power to repress and correct; but Paul knew that after his decease grievous wolves would enter in; yea, that of themselves perverse men would arise.   Peter assures us that the time was come for judgment to begin at the house of God.

We have seen that it had become, in the end of the second and in the third century, a common habit for the clergy, under pretext of purity—unmarried—to live and sleep with unmarried persons, consecrated also to celibacy as above all passion— above that evil matter into which pure souls were descended; for such was the doctrine of these mighty Alexandrians of which Dr. N. was enamoured.

Hermas, to whom I referred amongst others, alludes to it thus (the shepherd had commended him to the virgins who were there): "I said, 'Where shall I tarry?' They replied, 'Thou shalt sleep with us— as a brother, not as a husband; for thou art our brother, and we are ready henceforth to dwell with thee; for thou art very dear to us.' Howbeit, I was ashamed to continue with them. But she that seemed to be chiefest amongst them embraced me, and began to kiss me, and so did the rest. When the evening came on, I would forthwith have gone home; but they withheld me, and suffered me not to depart; therefore I continued with them that night near the same tower; so they spread their linen garments on the ground, and placed me in the middle; nor did they anything else— only prayed."

Origen complains bitterly of the great multitude of Christians who did not trouble themselves about divine things; and if they attended divine service, were entirely indifferent to it when there.

I add Cyprian's account. (A.D. 251.) He is accounting for the Decian persecution, and says it is only too light a chastisement, —"*exploratio potius quam persecutio videretur.*" All devoted to increasing their patrimony; no devoted religion in the priests, no upright faithfulness in ministers, no piety in works, no discipline in morals. Men's beards false, women's faces painted, eyes adulterated from what God had made them, their hair falsely coloured—cunning frauds to deceive the hearts of the simple. Artful deceit (*subdolæ voluntatis*) in circumventing brethren, marriages with unbelievers, prostituting to Gentiles the members of Christ; not only rash swearing, but perjury too; despising authority with haughty pretension; to speak evil with poisoned lip oneself; mutual discord with pertinacious hatred. Very many bishops, who should be an exhortation and example to others, despising their divinely-committed service (*divina procuratione*), make themselves agents (*procuratores*) of secular affairs, leave their see, desert the people, wandering through others' provinces, hunt after markets for gainful traffic, &c. (*De Lapsis*, 124. Fell's Ox. ed.)

Here is Jerome's account of the clergy. (A.D. 394.) "It is shameful to have to say, the priests of idols, buffoons, charioteers, harlots, receive inheritance; to the clergy and monks alone it is forbidden by law, and prohibited not by persecutors, but by Christian princes. Nor do I complain of the law, but that we should have deserved it. The cautery is good, but now the

worst is that I should need the cautery.
The provisions of the law are careful and
severe, and yet thus avarice is not re-
strained. We mock the laws by trustees.*
The glory of a bishop is to provide for
the wants of the poor. The disgrace of
all priests is the pursuit of their own
wealth. Born in a poor home, and in a
rustic hut, who could scarcely satisfy my
clamorous stomach with millet and the
coarsest bread, I now turn up my nose
at the finest flour and honey. I know
the kinds and names of fishes. I am
thoroughly *au fait* as to what shore shell
fish are found on. I discern the provinces
birds come from by their savour. I hear,
moreover, of the base service of certain
to old men and old women without
children. They put the chamber-pot

---

* Every one acquainted with English law is aware that
it was thus the statutes of mortmain were evaded. The
English lawyers thought it was invented here for this
purpose, but the clergy did not, it appears, want so long
to find it out.

beside the bed, take away with their own hand the purulent matter from the stomach, and phlegm of the lungs. They are full of fear at the arrival of the physician, and with trembling lips enquire if the patient is better; and if the old person is a little more vigorous they are in danger, and pretending falsely joy, the mind, inwardly avaricious, is tortured; for they fear lest they should lose their pains, and compare the living old body to the years of Methuselah." (*Epist. ad Nepotianum* lii. Vallarsii Ed. i. 261.)

Drunkenness, Augustine tells us, was universal; the clergy had lent themselves, he tells us, to the evil habits of heathens continuing among Christians in order to win and keep them. *He* did not (he was a godly faithful man), but put it down with danger to himself. (Epp. xxii. xxix. Ed. Ben.) It had reigned in other places (Ep. xxii.): he would have had the Africans set an example, but at any rate they should follow it.　These are his words in letter xxix. : "But lest they who preceded us, and permitted, or did not dare prohibit the manifest crimes of the inexperienced multitude, should seem to have some opprobrium cast on them by us, I explained to them by what necessity those things had arisen in the Church (getting drunk in church at the martyrs' festivals), namely, that when, after so many persecutions and so vehement, it would be a hindrance, when peace took place, to the crowd of Gentiles desirous of coming to the Christian name, that they were accustomed to pass festal days with their idols in abundance of feasts and drunkenness, nor could easily abstain from these very pernicious and yet very ancient pleasures : it seemed to those of old that they should spare for the time this part of infirmity, and celebrate not with like sacrilege, although with like luxury, other festal days after those which they had relinquished; that now, bound together as they were by the name of Christ, and subjected to the yoke of so great authority, salutary precepts of sobriety would be delivered to them, which, on account of the honour and fear of him who gave them, they would not be able to resist; as to which it was now time that, as those who did not dare deny their being Christians, they should begin to live according to the will of Christ, and that those things which were yielded to them that they might be Christians they should reject now they are so." Many said their fathers were good Christians, and did so. However, in that place Augustine succeeded. But here is a really holy man, the great light of the West, alleging that they had deliberately let the people be drunk in honour of martyrs, that they might not be so in honour of idols!

Gregory Thaumaturgus instituted saints' festivals to the same end, and Pope Gregory the first gave the same directions as to England. It was the same as to doctrine and worship. The Pagans did not attempt, says M. Beugnot (*Destruction du Paganisme*, ii. p. 271), to defend their altars against the progress of the worship of the mother of God. They opened to Mary the temples which they had kept shut against Jesus Christ, and avowed themselves conquered. He adds in a note, " Out of a multitude of proofs I shall choose one to show with what facility the worship of Mary swept before it the remains of Paganism which yet covered Europe. Notwithstanding the preaching of St. Hilarion, Sicily had remained faithful to the ancient worship. After the council of Ephesus (which decreed that Mary was the mother of God) we see its eight finest temples become in a very short time churches under the invocation of the virgin. Their temples were," &c., &c. "The annals of every country furnish like testimonies." "In truth," he continues, "they mixed with the adoration of Mary those Pagan ideas, those vain practices, those ridiculous superstitions, from which they seemed unable to separate themselves; but the Church rejoiced to see them enter within its bosom, because she well knew it would be easy for her, with the help of time, to purify from its alloy a worship which was purity itself." Thus some prudent concessions made temporarily to Pagan habits, and the influence exercised by the worship of the virgin, were the two elements of force made use of by the Church to conquer the resistance of the last Pagans.

It was the system. The Romans were passionately fond of festivals and processions. The Saturnalia and other feasts were at the end of December,—-Christmas* was fixed there. The Lupercalia in the end of January; it was a feast of purification,—the purification of the virgin Mary was fixed there. St. Peter de Vinculis replaced Augustus Cæsar, and so of many others. See Beugnot, ii. p. 263, &c., where the concessions to Pagan usages are enlarged on and justified. It is difficult to do this when they sanctified drunkenness by dedicating it to martyrs instead of demigods. M. Beugnot admits that their martyrs' festivals were a very large concession made to ancient manners, for all that passed while they lasted was little edifying! It was that system Vigilantius attacked and Jerome

---

* The feast now celebrated at Christmas (the very evergreens are Pagan) was the expression of one of the worst principles of heathenism—the reproductive power of nature, celebrated at the return of the sun from the winter solstice. The Hindoos celebrate their Uttarayana at this time—have their twelve days, sending of presents, and wishing many happy returns: so the heathen Romans, so the Teutonic nations. Compare Wilson's *Religious Festivals of Hindoos*, ii. p. 173.

defended. Christians went to the heathen feasts, as Augustine, Chrysostom, and many others testify; they resisted, as in the case of Pope Gelasius and others, and when Paganism fell and the populations entered in crowds, they gave them Christian festivals, so-called, to replace the heathen ones. It was a whole system.

I may take the passage I have referred to in Gregory Thaumaturgus' life by Gregory Nyssen, as describing it in the case of the former. I shall be excused these long quotations. It is the establishment of an immense system, paganising Christianity first in doctrines in Alexandria, then in ceremonies everywhere.* "But when with the divine help that tyranny had been overthrown, and peace had again accepted human life, service towards God, which lay before them, was free to every one according to his ability; descending

* The reader will find some other details on its establishment further on, connected with another subject.

again to the city, and going round the whole district in a circle, he made an appendage for the people everywhere to their divine service.   Having instituted the general assemblies for those who had been in the combat of faith, and, as they had taken away, different persons to different places, the bodies of the martyrs, going round in a procession, they celebrated festivities in a yearly anniversary, holding a general assembly to the honour of the martyrs.   For, indeed, this was a demonstration of his great wisdom, that, remodelling to a new life in a mass the whole generation of his day, set as a charioteer to nature, submitting them securely to the reins of faith and the knowledge of God, he allowed what was subject to the yoke of faith to caper a little in enjoyment.   For perceiving that the childish and uninstructed mind of the many remained, through bodily hilarity and enjoyments, in the error of idols, that the principal thing with them should be specially set right, their looking to God instead of vain objects for worship, he allowed them to make merry at the memories (tombs or places consecrated to them) of the martyrs, and to enjoy themselves and to celebrate festivities, that some time or other their life might be changed to what was more seemly and exact." It is said he left only seventeen heathen at his death.

But how opposite to the blessed delivering power of the Spirit, as seen in Scripture! How does it come under the apostle's word, "But now after that ye have known God, or rather are known of God, how turn ye again to the weak and beggarly elements, whereunto ye desire again to be in bondage? Ye observe days, and months, and times, and years. I am afraid of you, lest I have bestowed upon you labour in vain." This part of the history gives the decay in doctrine and spiritual state, till on the fall of Paganism its ceremonies and feasts were deliberately transferred to the nominal Church. Many went on with their heathenism. This was condemned by the hierarchical authorities, but long persevered in. Gregory I. condemns it in England, but directs, as Gregory Thaumaturgus did, similar feasts among the professing mass that had been brought in, to keep their fleshly minds contented. This was the Primitive Church, ante-Nicene and post-Nicene. From this we pass gradually into the mediæval. It was a space of nine hundred years, dark, confessedly dark, but we must leave it. Its result was what gave occasion to Protestantism. I shall examine the Church, and afterward the history of the popes. We shall see how far holiness, the alleged note of the Church, can be found.

In A.D. 953, 931–974, Ratherius, bishop of Verona and Liége, charges the clergy with corrupt avarice and universal incontinency; the popes themselves, many times married; a warrior, perjurer, heretic, gambler, and drunkard—such a shame to the whole Church—could not be a rebuker of others. He says in his Itinerary (Fleury, xii. p. 193) he held a synod to correct this, but the clergy kept none of the canons; the synods he held were to maintain the canons. There were bigamists, concubine keepers, conspirators, perjurers, drunkards, usurers. The cause of the ruin of all the people, he says, is the clergy. The ignorance of the clergy was excessive; he says they must learn the three creeds, and be able to read the gospel and certain services. No one, he says, was fit to be made a bishop, or to consecrate one. They would not give up their incontinency, and counted the rest for nothing. The Italian clergy despise the canons the most, because they are the most given to impudicity, and minister to this vice by ragouts and excess of

wine. (Dupin, vol. viii. p. 19, &c.   Fleury
l. c., from D'Achery and Mabillon.)   He
may have been said to be ruthless and
violent.   The Benedictines defend him.
Damianus, a great friend of Hildebrand
(Gregory VII.), the strictest of monks, re-
establisher, if not inventor, of the Flagel-
lators (self-scourgers), the able champion
of Rome against the Emperor, the reducer
of Milan (till then independent) to subjection to the pope, given up to devotion
to Mary, who gave up his cardinalate and
see to the great pain and offence of Hildebrand, out of piety, in a book entitled
" *Liber Gomorrhianus,*" the name of which
betrays its import, addressed to the pope,
complains of the way in which the clergy
were given up to such crimes, it being
alleged they could not depose them for it,
as people must have the sacraments : they
committed them, we read, with their own
children—I apprehend, those who came to
confession.   Pope Leo approved the book.

His letter of recommendation is prefixed
to it. Damianus refers to canons which
gave trifling penances for fornication; if
even with a nun, and habitually, five years'
penances. (These canons he alleged to
be forged, or of uncertain authority, though
amongst the canons.) Damianus demanded
the deposition of those guilty of these
things. The pope answers, they deserved
by the canons to be deposed, but out of
clemency he would depose only the most
immoral. On which Fleury remarks,
"Which leads us to suppose that the
numbers of the guilty were too great to
treat them with rigour." The next pope,
Alexander II., got the book and hid it,
of which Damianus complains bitterly.
In the Romish council of A.D. 1059,
he wished them to take it up; but it
was refused, as likely to produce scandal.
(Fleury, xii. 532; Dupin.)

Already, in A.D. 888, in two councils
(Mogunt. et Metens. Hardouin, vol. vi.),

the clergy are forbidden to have a mother or sister in the house, though it had been allowed.   In the latter case examples of vice had given occasion to it. (Conc. Mog., cap. x.)   Renolf of Soissons gave like orders. (889.)   In the council of Ænam-hense (1009), connection with women is forbidden; but it is added (ci.), "but it is worse that some should have two or more, and (*non-nullus*) such an one, although he had sent her off whom he lately had, during her life should marry another."

In the time of Gregory VI. (1045), Rome was full of assassins and robbers, says Fleury, quoting William of Malmes-bury.   They drew the sword even at the altar and the tombs of the apostles, to carry off the offerings as soon as they were put there, and use them for feasts, and to maintain corrupt women.   He exhorted, excommunicated in vain, and at last seized St. Peter's to begin, and drove away or killed those who were stealing the offerings.

In A.D. 910 and 927–941, Clugny (that is, the reformation of the monks) began. Before, in the confusion of the empire, laymen, women, had the monasteries as inheritances; abbots had their wives—as Campo, who had seven daughters and three sons, and his second, Hildebrand, and all their monks. Yet, in the well-known discourse of Bernard, abbot of Clairvaux, he says, the whole Christian people, from the least to the greatest, had conspired against God. It is not the time to say, As the people, so the priest; for the people are not even as the priest is. They are ministers of Christ, but serve Antichrist. All that remains is, that this Man of Sin should be revealed. (Sermon on Conversion of Paul.)

Pope Benedict VIII. rages against the licentiousness of the clergy (forbidding marriage), but more because the clergy, who were serfs, had children by free women, and the Church lost her property in serfs. Still, he declares, in language which I do not transfer to these pages, the universal and open profligacy of the clergy, more shameless than the laity. Between the years 1012 and 1014. (Hardouin, vi.)

It was at this epoch that the prohibition to the clergy to marry was rigidly enforced, and, as is known, by Hildebrand. The wives were treated as concubines by the popes; but they were married, and openly with ordinary solemnities very often. In England, it appears, few were not, but the kings made them pay for it. (Hard. Conc. Lon. vii. 1147.) Lanfranc allowed it; later, Anselm raged against it. It shows the state of Christendom, that many of the synods forbid the children born of the priests inheriting their cures. They gave them as portions even to their daughters. Paschal, pope, died A.D. 1118, ordered men on their death-beds to receive the sacrament from them, rather than from none ; and that their sons should be admitted to the priesthood in England, as almost the major part of the clergy, and the better part, were in this case. (Pascal's letter in Hard. vii. 1804–1807.) That the bishops took money for allowing the priests to live with women is recognized (Conc. Lat. cxiv., Hard. viii. 31),* and in the constitutions of Canterbury, where it is said, as spiritual judgments did not hinder the evil of con-cubinage, they were to be mulcted in their benefices.

Decrees as to this may be found in Hardouin, from 1217 to 1302 ; the canons of Conc. Lat. iv., 1215, enforced by Edmund, Archbishop of Canterbury, 1236, Hard. viii. 1236. In the canon law (*Distinct*. lxxxi. c., vi.) it is said, that a clergyman, convicted of having

* Thomas Aquinas counsels them to have a wife, secretly, or with connivance.

begotten children in the presbytery, is to be deposed. The gloss on this is—But it is generally said, that a clergyman is not to be deposed for simple fornication, because few can be found without that sin.

The literature of these ages teems with the bitterest reproaches against the clergy, as setting an example of simony, money-getting (one was alleged to have five hundred benefices), and licentious morals, brawls in taverns, unnatural crimes, impossible to be quoted, increased by a prohibition to marry, a measure not, however, fully carried into effect for two centuries, and long resisted in the north, as in England, Denmark, Norway, Sweden, the people often insisting that the priest should have a wife. Pope Alexander IV. (as quoted, it is not in Hardouin, and I have not access to Mansi) admits the evil state of things in 1258. "So a drowsiness of deadly carelessness seems in the greater part to have oppressed the vigilance of pastoral life, which we say, groaning, as the too great corruption of Christian people crying out from many regions testifies; which, when it ought to be cured by the remedies of a sacerdotal antidote, alas! grows greater by the contagion of evils, which proceeds from the clergy, so that it should be anywhere true what the prophetic complaint bears witness to, saying, As the people is become, so the priest."

I may now go on to a later state of things. The bishops received money regularly to allow the priests to keep women. This was forbidden by the council of Paris, 1429 (c. xxiii. Hard. vol. ix. Derlusanum (Tortosa), 1429, c. ii.; the council of Basle, session xx. c. i.). But it is said, it was again authorized by a local council of Breslau, that they were to put them away under a penalty of ten florins. I have not the German local councils to verify the quotation in this case.

Later again, W. F. Picus, Lord of Mirandola, that is the nephew of the famous Pic de Mirandola (as quoted in a literal extract which I cannot verify, not possessing his works) says, that priests left the natural use of women, and good boys were given up to them by their parents, and when grown older, then were made priests of. I give it literally, only in Latin : " Ab illis (sacerdotibus) etiam (proh pudor) fœminæ abiguntur ad eorum libidines explendas, et meritorii pueri a parentibus commendantur et condonantur his, qui ab omni corporis etiam concessa voluptate sese immaculatos custodire deberent. Hi postea ad sacerdotiorum gradus promoventur œtatis flore transacto jam exoleti." This was an address to pope Leo, in 1517, the year Luther began the Reformation.

The receiving of money by bishops for

priests' concubines was evidently general; complained of in Constance, written against by authors. Theodorich, Archbishop of Cologne, ordered them to be dismissed, and then took money from the priests for it. In the council of Paris, already quoted from Hardouin, they complain, that because of the concubinage of the clergy, with which many ecclesiastical and religious men (secular clergy and monks) are infected, the Church of God and the whole clergy are held in derision, abomination, and reproach by every body, and that most iniquitous crime has so prevailed in the Church of God, that Christians do not now believe simple fornication to be a sin. These testimonies may be multiplied *ad libitum.*

I go on now to what preceded the council of Pisa, a council that is a great trouble to Roman Catholics, as I may show further on. Clemangis was rector of the University of Paris, the most

famous then in the world, the corres-
pondent of popes and kings, earnestly
seeking the healing of the schism; for
there were two popes then. This led to
their using all possible means to make
money, provisions, annates, tenths, ex-
acting in every shape and every way,
giving a right to their favourites to a
living, whoever had a right to present to
it. He declares, that many of the clergy
did not know their A B C. He attacks
the cardinals for their pride and insolence;
though drawn from the lowest ranks of
the clergy, they had up to about five
hundred benefices. He says, "he is not
willing (*non volo*) to enumerate their
adulteries, rapts (*stupra*), fornications, by
which they pollute the Roman court, nor
relate the most obscene life of their family,
nothing inconsistent, however, with the
morals of their masters." The oppression
of the bishops was intolerable: if any
ecclesiastic was put in prison for any great

crime, on payment of a certain sum he came out as white as snow. He complains of the bishops, as we have seen they did, making the clergy compound for keeping a concubine. "If any now is lazy, if any one hates to work, he flies to the priesthood. As soon as he has attained to it, they diligently frequent brothels and taverns, and spend their time drinking, eating, dining, supping, playing at dice and games, gorged and drunken, they fight, cry out, make riots, execrate the name of God and His saints with their most polluted lips. *Sicque tandem compositi, ex meretricum suarum complexibus ad divinum altare veniuntur.*" This was a common complaint. "The bishops," he says, "go to court; perhaps they were better away, for what could they profit by their presence, who at the utmost enter the Church two or three times a year; who pass whole days in falconry and the chase, who eat most exquisite feasts, in shouting and dances, and pass their nights with girls and effeminate persons. Who drag by a base example the flock, by crooked paths, on to the precipice," &c. Were the monks and councils better? They are pharisees, false doctors, the ravening wolves spoken of in Scripture; he calls the nunneries brothels of Venus. To make a girl take the veil is to give her up to prostitution. All that Dupin ventures to say as to this last is, that he describes it in very strong terms, and apparently too violent (*outrés*).

Clemangis admits that there are exceptions to this state of the clergy, but that the majority are such. Now, I do not doubt a moment that there were godly men who shrunk away from all this iniquity, and sought communion with God, some persecuted, some not; and communities of another character, not under vows, as the brethren of the common doctrine, Groot, Thomas à Kempis, and many others, whose schools merged in the light of the Reformation. But this is the character of the so-called Holy Catholic Apostolic Church. Christian conscience, yea, natural conscience, was weary of the wickedness.

I shall be told that the *doctrine* of the Church was holy. Dr. Milner's book, a standard one in England, tells us, that there is the doctrine of holiness, the means of holiness, the fruits of holiness, the divine testimony of holiness. That the Church itself was holy,* he does not attempt to

---

* Dr. Pusey tells us, in defending himself against Romanizers, that it is by faith the Church is recognized as holy. What a confession! And note—holiness is one mark by which we are to recognize the true Church (a doctrine I do not except to) ; but when we come to seek it as a mark, then we must believe it to be holy, by means of faith. What a satire! What are we to believe to be holy? the unholy Church? And how is it then a proof? I am to know the true Church by its holiness, and when I find an awfully wicked body, believe it is holy because it is the Church. I must say this is a mockery, and a mockery in holy things ; a trifling with the claims of God.

show; he speaks of individuals, a number of persons who have given their names to churches as saints, and besides that, it was certain, there have been a countless number. As to sanctity of doctrine, he speaks of the Trinity and the Incarnation, &c., most holy doctrines surely, but not doctrines about holiness. He identifies justification and sanctity, saying, "the efficient cause of justification or sanctity" —the principal and most efficient means being the sacraments, and then her public service. The attestation of sanctity is miracles.

Now, there is not an attempt to say that the Church is holy; in fact, I do not admit the doctrines of Rome to be holy. It is not holy to confound sanctity and justification; it is not holy to make sacraments the principal means, leaving out the Word and Spirit of God, to which Christ and His apostles directly ascribe sanctification. It is not holy, it is Mani-

cheism to make holiness, and a holiness
necessary to the clergy, by a prohibition
to marry. It was the most unholy and
wicked doctrine against which the apostle
warns us, as a doctrine of devils, the fruit
of a conscience seared with a hot iron.
The fruits of it have been produced.
They characterized the Church. If a man
can devote himself to the Lord, body,
soul, and spirit, without a snare to himself,
be it so. It is a grace and gift from God.
But the moment you *forbid* to marry, you
are on Manichean and Gnostic ground.
It is urged, in order to defend Rome,
that the passages in Paul's epistle to
Timothy apply to Gnostics. I admit it.
They held that matter was a bad thing,
hence that Christ had no material body,
and other extravagancies of every kind;
but as a way or means of holiness, they
taught abstinence from women. This was
the doctrine of the Alexandrian school
Dr. N. admires. They were infected with

it. The Albigenses, the mediæval fruit of Gnosticism in Christendom, constantly practised it; their perfect (or *bonshommes*,) did not eat meat, nor have to say to women.

The Roman Catholic Church taught holiness in this way, and of this kind. Their doctrine was unholy, what the fruits of it were we have seen. Further, the doctrine of indulgences was a horribly unholy doctrine. We are told it is only the remission of the temporal punishment of sin. But if a man died with the sacraments, he never could have any other. It was purgatory that was feared. A good Catholic has nothing else to fear; besides, the ignorant masses were not so nice as to this. The terror of sin was on their consciences, and the Roman Church helped them to get rid of this terror; not by Christ's blood for the repentant, known by faith, and therefore purifying; not by having their soul restored by the operation of the Spirit of God, but by pardons bought with money. It was used to build and adorn churches, farmed out to bankers. A money tariff was made for sins, or the commutations of them, and years, thousands of years, of purgatory avoided by paying money. It was a traffic of sin—security as to future sins, too. The nominal Church had returned to Pagan vices, as Paul foretold it would. (Compare Rom. i. and 2 Tim. iii.) The difference was this: corruption had its way in Paganism; it was horrible as horrible could be. But Papal Rome systematized it, and made a tariff for sin! Not in the known world, that I am aware of, has there been iniquity like this—a tariff made for sin! Can Dr. N. be surprised that there arose a protest against it? that there were Protestants?

The word of God was brought out; no one can deny it. Old truths were maintained, and justification by faith preached.

Truth was preached. That man's will, long suppressed, broke out; that the Church was not set up as at the beginning, I admit; that a vast mass of Protestantism has fallen into infidelity, alas! I do not deny, though in Germany there is a strong reaction, and it is *far more the case* among cultivated Roman Catholics, only they do not publish it, as in Germany. But a protest against Rome could not have been delayed. It had been going on at Pisa, at Basle, at Constance, by legal attempts, by the *centum gravamina*, by the complaints of Bernard and Wessalas, and holy men of times previous to the Reformation. All the difference was, that God then raised up men of sufficient faith to brave the pope; whereas previously the reformation had been left to the popes, and all was worse than ever.

I admit and feel that it is dismal work going over all this wickedness; and I have still to pursue the task. If we pursue the study of the truth, it nourishes and sanctifies. We are occupied with unseen things; but as the imagination of men is sought to be filled with an idea of the Holy Catholic Church, it is needful to turn to the facts, that one may know that what is called the Catholic Church was the most unholy thing in the world—that it had extinguished the truth, put to death the saints, and corrupted morals till it became intolerable. Satan was not allowed to set aside the dogmatic foundation of the evidence of a divine Saviour, as in the mass of the population in the East by Mohammedanism; so that still I do not the least doubt many unknown pious souls were found, and some known, however dark in knowledge, as Bernard; but these felt the evil. As Bernard said, it only remained for Antichrist to come.

My object here is not to go through the Roman Catholic controversy; when God's word is believed it is very simple.

Hebrews ix. and x. suffice to prove it apostate in its central doctrine. I believe it false in all that distinguishes it. Its pretension to catholicity is absurd, as probably the majority of Christendom, and certainly the most ancient churches, are outside its pale. Unity hence fails in its first element. There is no external unity now. Nor was there in the Roman body in former times. The great modern doctrine of the immaculate conception of the Virgin Mary was denied by the most powerful body in the Roman system, the Dominicans. The prince Archbishop of Breslau left that system not long ago because of its being papally decreed.* Transubstantiation was only decreed in A.D. 1215, having been rejected by the best of the fathers and doctors for centuries: the contrary doctrines were used earnestly by them against the

---

* Dr. Pusey, in his *Eirenicon*, has fully shewn what Dr. Newman's statement as to the unanimity of modern Romanists on this point is worth.

Eutychians. Whatever apostolic succession is worth, it is far more elsewhere than at Rome. But I cannot enter now into all these questions. I am accounting for the Protestantism which Dr. N. hated.

It will be alleged that there was individual sanctity. Now, that there were God's hidden ones in all times I cannot doubt a moment. And if the character of their holiness shewed want of scriptural light, it was not necessarily the less sincere. Still, it is beyond all question, that the universal unholiness of the professing world, and especially of the priests, and the idolatry prevalent in Christendom, exposed those whose consciences were oppressed by what was all around them to fall into the snares laid for them by Satan in the shape of false doctrine. The effect of this was, that Christendom was composed of, first, unholy, iniquitous, and persecuting orthodoxy (a few souls groaning under the state of things, such as Bernard, who said, All that remained was for Antichrist to come; and others, that he was born already at Rome); secondly, of a vast number (for they filled the country from Asia to Spain) who had fallen into Manichean notions, and sought holiness by judging all matter as itself unholy, but whose devoted and blameless walk won the conscience of the population, till they were put down by fire and sword; and thirdly, of a number—whose doctrines it is hard to discover—whose constancy and blameless walk astonished conscientious men; and lastly, of others who were counted only schismatics, whose only fault was that they could not own the corruption which reigned around them. One class or another of these was spread all over Europe. It is a sad history; for they were all hunted as wild beasts all over the country, burned and tortured, and it is often hard to ascertain what they really did hold. The inquisition was

invented for putting them down. Of one
large class, Albigenses and Waldenses (of
whom the former, I suppose, were, as to
their leaders at any rate, more or less
Manichean), the judgments at Toulouse
may be found in the end of Limborch's
History of the Inquisition, other notices
in many popular books, and a good deal
of research as to them collected in a note
to Elliott's *Horæ Apocalypticæ*. Of the
Moravians, before they were driven out of
Bohemia and Moravia, the best account is
a German work—*History of the Bohemian
Brethren*—by Gindely.* Prague, 1857.

But I must add a few words as to the
character of the holiness that was introduced as the Church declined, and when
it had lost its first love and true Christian
holiness of walk. We have seen, by con-

---

* "Geschichte der Böhmischen Brüder." Part of a
larger work. "Böhmen u. Mähren, im Zeitalter der
Reformation." Gindely is a Romanist; but fair enough
as a historian.

temporary statements of Cyprian, Jerome, Augustine, that this was the case, and dreadfully so. I now only notice the character of what was substituted. It was at a time (and it is not without importance to note it) when Jerome complains bitterly that there was no need to make laws against heathen priests and deceivers, but that there was against Christian priests besetting the sick-beds of old persons in order to get their inheritance. A new kind of sanctity was introduced — devotedness to the saints, monastic habits of life, celibacy, &c. Jerome, Paulinus of Nola, and Martin of Tours, were the great promoters of this. Sulpicius Severus gives us the history of the last, Jerome and Paulinus furnish us with their own history; but it was a spurious holiness, false miracles and wonders, accompanied with drunkenness and violent tempers. No one can deny that the men I have named were the types and promoters of this kind of devotion.

Let us see some of the historical characteristics of it. First, as to Martin of Tours, the apostle of Gaul. He lay on ashes, as he was, for his bed, and covered with a sack and the like; and when he put his foot out of the cell to go a couple of miles to church, all the possessed in the church shewed he was coming, though in different ways, so that the clergy learnt thus he was coming. "I saw" (I quote from Sulp. Sev. Dialogues iii. 6) "one caught up into the air as Martin was coming—suspended on high, with his hands stretched out, his feet unable to touch the ground: Martin prayed prostrate in sackcloth and ashes. Then you might see the unhappy men cleansed by their going out in different ways; these, their feet being carried up on high, hang as if from a cloud, and yet their garments not fall down over their face, lest the naked part of their bodies should put people to shame."

So in Egypt. Two friends went to see one of the Anchorites. An enormous lioness came and sought him, and they all followed her. She took them to a cave, and they saw what was the matter: five cubs were all blind. The Anchorite stroked their eyes, and they saw. Soon after the lioness brought a skin of some rare wild beast—how acquired we do not learn—and brought it to the Anchorite, and he took it and wore it. (Dialogue i. 9.) Another lived up in Mount Sinai, naked; and, when at last seen, he said, He who was visited by men, could not be by angels.

Martin met a furious cow that had gored several. She was rushing at him. He told her to stand, and she did; and then saw a devil on her back, and ordered him off; and he went, and the cow was quiet. Nor was that all. The cow knew very well what had happened, and came and

knelt down before Martin, then, on Martin's
order, went and found the herd. (Dialogue
ii. 9.)   He was most familiar with demons ;
knew when it was Jupiter, when Mercury,
who was the most troublesome of all, and
specially when he had the saints with him.
When Sulp. Sev. went to see him all was
harmony, and Martin was talking, and
women's voices within, for two hours,
while Sulpicius and Gallus were outside.
This turned out, as he told them after he
came out covered with ashes and filth,
to be Agnes, and Thecla, and Mary :
often Martin said Peter and Paul ; but
then all of a sudden a whole lot of devils
came, Martin denouncing them by their
names.   Jove, he said, was a brute, and
stupid (*brutum et hebetum*).   Alas ! they
beset his dying bed. (Letter iii. to
Bassula.)   "Why are you standing there,
bloody beast ?" he said ; "thou shalt find
nothing, O fatal one, in me ; the bosom
of Abraham has received me ;" and so

expired.   Yet he had promised pardon to the devil if he repented.   The devil was accusing some monks who had sinned after baptism.   Martin replied that crimes were purged by the conversation of a better life, and God would pardon ; and then said to the devil, if he, as judgment-day was near, even then left off following after men, and repented of his deeds, he himself, trusting in the Lord, promised him the mercy of Christ.   I might multiply all kinds of stories, but this surely is enough ; he died A.D. 402, or thereabouts.   When he dined with the Emperor, he gave the cup to the Presbyter first, as superior to him ; such was the lowliness of the ascetic worker of miracles. (Life, xxiii.)

This was the kind of sanctity now introduced.   Paulinus's was specially shewn in honouring St. Felix.   He had festivals in honour of his saint.   But, alas! as we have seen, this change to honouring saints instead of heathen demigods, thus syste-

matically established, did not change
the habits.   He deplores the votaries
honouring the saints with drinking bouts.
*Verum utinam sanis agerent hoc gaudia
votis, nec sua liminibus miscerent pocula
sanctis. (Natalis,* 9.)   So elsewhere.*   He
adds, he has covered St. Felix's house
with holy pictures; that the gaper may
drink in sobriety, and forget too much
wine.   He implores the aid of St. Felix
directly, not even his intercession, for
sickness and a bad eye; he calls himself
him that is thine; he seems to make the

* However, he thinks such joys are to be pardoned, as
error creeps into rude minds ; nor, conscious of so great
a fault, fails in piety in fancying amiss the saints' delight
in it.

——— Ignoscenda tamen puto talia parvis,
Gaudia quæ ducunt epulis, quia mentibus error
Irrepit rudibus, nec tantæ conscia culpæ,
Simplicitas pietate cadit, male credula Sanctos
Perfusis halante mero gaudere sepulcris.

Is this holiness—is it a system of holiness? Paulinus
does not approve of it.   But it was common ; and the
system which gave rise to it was approved by Rome, as a
system.   In the well-known letter to Mellitus, Gregory I.

M

saints particularly efficacious wherever a part of their body was.   This is the holiness Baronius compares with Protestantism.   (394, xciii.)

As to St. Jerome, it is impossible to have a more eloquent description of Romish holiness than the efforts of the excellent Tillemont to keep poor Jerome's name among the saints.   He sought to overcome his nature, I dare say.   He fasted excessively, lived in grime and filth, did everything possible to subdue flesh by flesh's efforts ; but nature is not overcome

desires Augustine not to pull down the temples, if well built, but to sprinkle them with holy water, put relics of saints in them, and as they were accustomed to slaughter many oxen in the sacrifice of demons, the solemnity was to be changed somewhat.   On the festival of the saint whose relics were there, they were to make booths about the cleansed temple, and celebrate the solemnity with religious feasts ; that while some external joys were reserved to them, they might be better able to consent to internal ones, as it was not doubtful it was impossible to cut off all, at once, with hard minds.   He cites Jewish sacrifices as a condescension to heathen habits in Egypt. (Lib. ix. 71, or xi. 76.)

thus. Tillemont declares that he was very little exact in stating things as they were, following more his own ideas than the truth. These, however, he says, are the defects of a great genius. But he did not weigh what he said, and, which is more to be regretted, attacked St. Chrysostom; indeed, whoever he had as an adversary was the basest of men : he had too great an idea of his eloquence, shews it, was naturally jealous and envious, so as to wound his greatest friends and alienate them. It is hard not to recognize that he had in his natural character a sourness and bitterness which pained many. He was soon on fire when offended, and did not easily pardon. Are we to say, he asks, if so many saints who have admired him, and the Church who honours him amongst its saints and doctors, have been deluded —a humble son of the Church cannot say that—St. Ambrose, St. Chrysostom, St. Augustine are excellent models of a perfect virtue to animate us to imitate them? But others have had great sins, as David. We may say, even, that the defects of Jerome are useful, as teaching us what the substance (*le fond*) of virtue and Christian piety is. For if it consisted in an even and uniform life, in which few faults are committed, one would have to prefer Rufinus to him. But the Church leaves him to God's judgment, and has always had the greatest respect for Jerome. Not the services he has rendered the Church by his labours;* these are not virtues.

Tillemont can see that in his case his austerities would not do. Doubtless, he says, they were very useful to him (which his own account by-the-by does not shew, though I do not question their sincerity in seeking to maintain incorruptness in celibacy, which he held the highest of virtues), yet, if we had nothing else to

* He corrected the translation of the Scriptures.

praise in him, we should have reason to fear they had rendered him proud, and had been the cause of that severe and critical spirit which some have blamed in him. He then shews what he thinks proof of what constitutes a saint : first, his love of his solitary life and poverty, though he could have enjoyed the favour of Pope Damasus and the wealth of Saint Marcella and Saint Paula, two rich women who admired him greatly ; and his fleeing those who honoured him—humility which was shewn in not exercising the functions of priest, for which he had been brought up ; his eleemosynary charity and laborious service for others, when he might have been glad to be writing ; he hopes, his anger against his heretical adversaries, and certainly his conduct in exalting St. Augustine, when he might have seemed a competitor, the more so as he had quarrelled with him.

Such is Tillemont's kindly and gracious

excuse for what he was obliged to tell in his history; for, in fact, Jerome's language, particularly against those who deprecated monkish sanctity, saint and image worship, was regular *Billingsgate*; for that is really the only word to describe it by. Tillemont then makes a saint of him in these words. " The Scripture does not call him alone happy who is without spot and does not sin ; but, moreover, him to whom God does not impute sin, because he hates it by a pure and sincere love of righteousness, and that he covers it by the nuptial robe of charity, which covers a multitude of sins "—a deep and deadly error, arising from a confusion of Proverbs x. 12, quoted by Peter, and Psalm xxxii. 1.   I believe, as to God's government in the Church, fervent charity may keep many sins out of sight by Christian forgiveness, so as not to come before God for present judgment ; but to confound it with Psalm xxxii., quoted in Romans iv., is a denial of the gospel and the truth, but the foundation of Romish righteousness and sanctity, even in the hands of the very respectable Tillemont.

Another painful question may be asked, Why bring all this failure up, if things are changed ? Is there such vice now ? In the first place I reply in the enquiry, Has the Romish body the " note of holiness " ? the facts are everything. It certainly has not. But I must answer. There is no doubt that the light and spiritual energy of the Reformation caused a certain amelioration in Rome ; but I still must say, that where the action of this is not directly felt, it is not changed. Mr. Froude, whose hard-riding imagination had made a picture of mediæval holiness, as we learn, was checked by the degeneracy he found in Italy. We have seen what they degenerated from. I have known a good deal by personal experience in several countries, and a good deal more by that of others; and I believe that in principle and practice there is no change, though there may be more concealment. It is thought infidelity is found among Protestants especially. It is a mistake: more, I believe, in the bosom of what is called Catholicism; but not published, as among those called Protestants. Go to France and Italy, and see the state of men, in towns especially.

I turn to the Popes, to see what their history affords as a stay to the soul, or if it were a cause of righteous revolt. The absence of the Emperors from Rome, and their presence at Constantinople, made the Episcopate of Rome a post of great importance and political power. Its ecclesiastical jurisdiction was really comparatively small. It was respected as the See of the capital, and had a primary rank —if worldly rank is to be looked for in Christ—which Constantinople contested with it as the new capital. But Augustine, the great Western doctor, and the African council, forbad appeals to Rome as intolerable.   But I confine myself here to their history, that we may have what we are called to look upon as infallible, as commanding our respect and submission as holy, as of God.

Already, in the fourth century, intrigues for the possession of Papal power became a source of public trouble.   In A.D. 366 Pope Liberius died, and contests for the See began.   Damasus was elected by a majority, Ursicinus by a large party—both were consecrated Bishops of Rome. The Emperor banished Ursicinus; but his partisans met in the churches they possessed, and refused communion with Damasus.   The Emperor took away the churches.   They met outside Rome, and were banished the country. In the dispute, the parties fought for victory, and a vast number of Christians were killed, even in the churches.

But the origin of the violent feud is more important than the feud itself. The Emperor Constans was an Arian persecutor. Liberius had condemned Athanasius, and communicated with the Arians. When called on to subscribe an Arian creed, it appears he repented, and recalled his condemnation. The Emperor summoned a council at Arles, where the legates of Liberius signed a semi-Arian creed. Afterwards, at the council of Milan, hesitating, he was banished, and Felix consecrated Pope by an Arian minority. Rome murmured, and Liberius was restored, after three years' exile; but signed an Arian creed; and there were two Popes —one said to be really Arian, and in communion with Arians who had made him Pope; the other, who had signed an Arian creed against his conscience. Felix was driven out by the people, who favoured Liberius, though the clergy had mainly submitted to Felix. Liberius wrote

to the Eastern Bishops, who had condemned Athanasius, to declare his agreement with them, and that he never agreed
with Athanasius. Osius, of Cordova, the
president of the council of Nice which
condemned Arius, had given way to the
emperor before Liberius. Felix is counted
among the Popes as Felix II. Damasus
was of the Felix party, and hence the
riots. It is stated, that in the riots about
Felix, which were very great, many were
killed; that there were real massacres in
baths, streets, and churches, of laity and
clergy who favoured Felix; but there is
some obscurity as to the history. (Bar.,
Anno 357, Tillemont, vol. vi.; Hilarii P.
Fragmenta, p. 1335, where he interrupts
his history, or rather Liberius' letter to the
Eastern bishops, and turns to anathematize
Liberius.) Efforts have been made to
screen Liberius, by questioning what
Sirmian creed he adopted. So Baronius.
But, if we are to trust Hilary, there can

be no mistake as to his Arianism; nor does Tillemont nor Dupin defend him from this accusation, nor Jerome either.

Zosimus became Pope A.D. 417. He formally approved Pelagianism. The synod at Lydda accepted Pelagius' confession of faith. Augustine and the African bishops had condemned him. Zosimus reproves them sharply. The African churches met A.D. 418; Pelagius was condemned and anathematized; and they add, if any one presumed to appeal beyond sea, no one was to receive him into communion. There is as to what follows some conflict of dates; but a decree of the Emperor Honorius was obtained, Pelagius and Cœlestius banished from Rome, and Zosimus now condemned what he had approved, and cut them both off from communion. On the death of Zosimus (A.D. 418), two Popes, Boniface and Eulalius, were elected. Boniface attempted to maintain his place by force. The Prefect kept the peace, and reported in favour of Eulalius to the Emperor Honorius. Honorius confirmed Eulalius, and banished Boniface from the city. Boniface maintained his ground outside, and his partisans appealed to Honorius. The Emperor cited both before him. The Prefect told him neither could be trusted in their statements. Difficulties arose in the decision. Honorius forbade both to go into the city, and sent a Bishop for the Easter ceremonies. However, Eulalius went in. His adherents were unarmed. Boniface's, who were of the populace, made a violent attack, and the Prefect hardly escaped. But Honorius, glad to terminate the matter, condemned Eulalius for going in, and appointed Boniface. Eulalius was driven out of the city by force. (*Baronius' Annals*, 419.)

It was about this time that the Popes alleged forged canons of the council of Nice to maintain their authority in Africa. The African Bishops had the records of

Constantinople, Antioch, and Alexandria, besides their own, searched; found they were forged, and refused to submit, reproving Pope Celestine, and denying his right to send his Legate *a latere.* These appeals of evil persons the Popes were constantly receiving as a means of establishing their authority. (*Hardouin's Councils*, i. 934, Prohibition to Appeal, Can. 125, Letters to Pope Boniface, 939, and to Celestine, 947.) The letter to Celestine is very strong indeed. Faustinus the Legate's mission being wholly rejected.

The fifth general council condemned three chapters of the fourth. Pope Vigilius, who was at Constantinople, had demanded the council called the fifth; then objected to it, and would not assist; was exiled by the Emperor, published a constitution condemning the chapters, saving that he did not condemn the council of Chalcedon (the fourth), on whose authority they rested. The Romans wished him back. The Emperor agreed, and said they might have him or Archdeacon Pelagius for Pope, or the latter after Vigilius. They wished Vigilius, and said they would take Pelagius afterwards, as he prescribed to them, and the Emperor let him go, on his confirming the council which condemned the three chapters. He died in Sicily on the way. Pelagius, who was suspected of poisoning him, succeeded him; publicly declaring, however, his innocence. Vigilius himself had climbed over the wall into the Papacy, Belisarius having, by the Empress' orders, sent off Pope Silverius, who would not submit to the Emperor's theology, and put in Vigilius. Silverius, however, returned. Belisarius gave him up to Vigilius, who sent him to the island Palmaria, in guard, where he died. (*Fleury*, 537–558; vol. vii. 356, 482.) Baronius (sub an. 538) counts Silverius Pope till his death. Vigilius had promised two hundred pounds of gold to Belisarius, and would not pay it. Pelagius' own election was very uncertain. Vigilius had at first condemned the three chapters in his *judicatum.* Thereupon the Roman clergy separated from him. The Africans excommunicated him. He, seeing he had condemned thus a general council to please the Emperor, and that the clergy turned against him, retracted; but meanwhile, it seems (Conf. *Pagi ad. Bar.* 555, viii. note), the Roman clergy elected Pelagius. Then Vigilius yielded, and got into favour again, and the Emperor told the Romans they might have which they liked, and Pelagius, who came back with Vigilius from Constantinople, certainly joined in ill-treating him. Baronius says, no day or month is named when he succeeded, and complains bitterly of all this. Vigilius had condemned the council of Chalcedon, and written to the three other Patriarchs (who were heretics according to it), anathematized the doctrines of the council of Chalcedon, and Pope Leo in his famous letter adopted by it, and renounced communion with those who defended it. Baronius denies the authenticity of these letters; but Pagi and Fleury both admit they are genuine. Silverius was really murdered by want and starvation. "He died of hunger," says Fleury; and indeed all historians remark that Vigilius was chosen Pope when Silverius was alive, and never afterwards. Baronius tries to get out of it by supposing Vigilius was re-elected after Silverius' death; but it is merely because it ought to be. Silverius was son of Pope Hormisdas. (*Fleury* and *Baronius* 53, cxxi.) Vigilius ordained eighty-one Bishops.

Pope Honorius was condemned as a heretic by the sixth œcumenical council. Baronius laboriously seeks to prove that Theodoret did it, and left his own name out, and put Honorius' in; but Pagi, his

N

annotator, has, in very few words, and by
facts, shown the absurdity of his attempt.
Pope Adrian II. refers to it, and says
heresy was the only ground for resisting
thus such a superior authority. He was
anathematized also by Pope Leo II. (See
Fleury, xl. 28. For the acts of the
council, see *Hardouin*; quoted in *Baronius*
and *Fleury*.)

Symmachus and Laurentius contended for
the Papacy. (A.D. 498.) It was a violently
contested matter. Both were ordained
Pope the same day, and they appealed to
Theodoric at Ravenna, Gothic king, an
Arian, to decide. As most were for
Symmachus, he was to be Pope. He was
accused of all sorts of crimes, and never
was cleared. There was fighting in the
streets for a length of time, and many
killed and wounded. The only godly
man we hear of was on the other side.
Symmachus made regulations to hinder
these contests. In vain, however; for

men will be ambitious. The clergy had in other cases sold all the churches' goods, and even the vessels of service, by auction, for pushing their candidates; so that it had been forbidden by rescripts and laws of the senate; and after Vigilius' election more than 3000 *solidi* were not to be paid at court after an election for the royal confirmation, &c., for a Pope; 2000 for a Metropolitan. This was in A.D. 532. The king wrote to John, the new Pope, recalling a decree of the senate in the previous Pope's time, and allows his officers to take so much. (*Fleury*, book vii. 625.)

The history of the Papal influence was this—when there were Emperors, they ruled; but the Pope's influence was growing ecclesiastically, though often resisted. When the empire fell they were the chief influence (except the Arian Goths in Italy), and did pretty freely what they pleased, increasing in power in respect of Constantinople. However, the Gothic

Kings confirmed them, and interfered, and were appealed to, as we have seen. When for a time the eastern empire reconquered Italy, the Popes were servile and submissive to the Emperors : could not help it. When these were driven out again, they were oppressed by Lombards, but established in Rome by the Franks ; Charlemagne, however, fully holding his own, and ruling at Rome. When the succeeding Carlovingian Emperors were weak and divided, their power grew. Powerful Emperors contended for the right of confirmation of Popes and local investiture of Prelates ; and the history of the middle ages is the history of this conflict. The Popes raising Italy against them (Guelphs and Ghibelines), and the Emperors sometimes doing as they pleased ; but the German Emperors having to contend with subject Princes as powerful as themselves, and jealous of them, the Pope and they coalesced against the Emperors : the

Popes even supported the rebellion of a son against his father the Emperor.

In Boniface the eighth's time they laid their hands on France; but this was more united, and there was a signal failure. The Pope had to give way. The next Pope had his seat at Avignon, under French influence—the Avignon Popes and the court being degraded to the last degree. At the end they had one Pope at Rome and another at Avignon, this giving rise to the question whether the authority of a council were not superior to that of a Pope, and the three councils of Pisa, Basle (Florence, Lausanne), and Constance, which so puzzle Roman Catholic theorists. There was a universal cry for reformation in head and members, always avoided. At last came the Reformation, which threw the whole power into the Pope's hand, the Bishops holding only under him. And though Louis XIV. maintained Gallican liberties, as they are called, yet the clergy are simply slaves to the Pope. The Jesuit society sprung up at that time, more powerful than the Pope himself, and recovered southern Germany to Popery.

I have now to see in what way the state of the Papacy gave occasion to Protestantism. From A.D. 887, then, the Popes were engaged in the strifes of the Italian nobles, when the power of the Empire fell. Another circumstance has to be introduced here. A number of forged decretals were produced at this time, which formed the foundation of the Popes' pretensions subsequently—the Isidorean collection. No doubt political circumstances were a means of the Popes' power, but their canonical pretensions leaned on these forged decretals. They declare the notable falsehood that all churches had their origin from Rome—"*A quâ omnes ecclesias principium sumsisse*"—and then go on to state its consequent rights. It is said they were written between A.D. 829

and A.D. 845; appear at Mentz in the time of Archbishop Autcarius; alleged to be brought from Spain at the end of the eighth century, or thereabouts. Some think they were forged by Autcarius himself, at Mentz; and that there were some old decretals which gave rise to them, or as some allege, introduced to accredit the forgeries. At any rate, what gave legal (not political) force to Papal authority from this date, was the forged Isidorean collection. It is admitted, on all hands, they are forgeries. They were not detected till the Reformation. Calvin states it (Inst. iv. 7, 20, and the Cent. ii. 7) and fully (iii. 7) demonstrated it. Bellarmine says they are ancient, but does not dare defend them as genuine; and Baronius gives them up. (vi. 865, and following, with Pagi Ann.) Hincmar combatted, in A.D. 870, the authority of the decrees, but used them too. However, no one denies their spuriousness, but they served their purpose when wanted. They were used by Nicholas I. in A.D. 864.

I turn to the history of the Popes from this time. After the death of Formosus (A.D. 897), Boniface took possession of the See, and held it for fifteen days. Stephen VI. (VII.) drove him out and took possession. Baronius here remarks : Boniface is not to be counted, Stephen is ; future Popes having owned one, not the other, the clergy thought it better, though all was taken by fear and violence, to sanction it, rather than by electing a legitimate Pope to have a schism. (Bar. i. 897.) Stephen dragged Formosus out of his tomb, clothed him in pontifical robes, and put him on the throne ; charged him with intrusion into the See (he had been made Pope in a tumult, Sergius having been chosen by a party), stripped him then of his pontifical robes, cut off the three fingers which were used to bless with, and had his body thrown into the

Tiber, and re-ordained all the clergy he had ordained. Baronius says he should not dare to count him among the Popes, if he had not found it done by those of old. (vi. 987.) Stephen was put in prison and strangled. Baronius owns he had only the fact of subsequent recognition by the Church to accept such a Pope. (i. 897.)

I should have, perhaps, mentioned the history of Pope Joan. A woman, an English woman, who had received a learned education at Athens, became, it is said, Pope A.D. 855. She is said to have died in child-birth, having been taken with pains of labour in the street, going to the Lateran Church; so that the Popes never pass that way. That seems unquestionable, and it is certain that the sex of the Pontiffs was examined for long years, and the story believed till the time of the Reformation—that is, for many centuries. She is put by Platina, who speaks of the story as of uncertain authority,

between Leo IV. and Benedict III.
The whole controversy is fully gone into
in Basnage, vii. 12, and Schröck, xxii.
75–110.   Baronius and Fleury pass the
Joan of Platina over in a suspicious
silence, and make Benedict elected on the
death of Leo IV.   Here, too, there was
a contested election : Anastasius was
chosen by the people, and installed Pope,
Benedict by the clergy, and Anastasius
was driven away.

To continue.   After Stephen was gone,
the Roman faction having the upper hand
at the time, Romanus was Pope somewhat
more than four months. I quote Baronius's
account : " Thus, indeed, all things, as
well sacred as profane, were mixed up with
factions, so that promotion to the Apostolic
See of the Roman Pontiff was in the
power of the party which seemed the
strongest. So that at one time the Roman
nobles, at another the Prince of Etruria,
intruded by secular power whom he would,

and put down, when he could, the Roman
Pontiff promoted by the contrary faction.
Which things were carried on for almost a
whole century, until the Othos (German
Emperors) came in between, in opposition
to both parties, but arrogating to themselves in the same way the election of a
Pope, and his deposition when elected."
Romanus disappeared. Theodorus was
Pope twenty days. Benedict IV. succeeded,
of whom nothing is known; he seems
to have been a respectable man. Leo V.
succeeded. After forty days he was driven
out, and put in prison by Christopher.
He was, after seven months, driven out,
put in prison, and obliged to retire to a
monastery by Sergius, who was all-power-
ful through Adelbert, Marquis of Tuscany.

It is to be added, that these Popes undid
the ordinations of their predecessors, as
having no legitimate title. One Auxilius
wrote a dialogue, to guard, by decrees and
canonical examples, against the intestine

discord of the Roman Church; namely, on ordinations, exordinations, and super-ordinations. (*Baronius*, 907, iii.) "That reprobate Sergius," says Baronius (908, ii.), "the slave of all vices, the most iniquitous of all men—what did he leave un-attempted?" "One Pope undid," he says, "all the acts of another; what, then (912, vii.), was the face of the holy Roman Church? how filthy, when the most powerful and basest harlots ruled at Rome! at whose will Sees were changed, Bishops given, and, what is horrible and unutterable to hear of, their lovers were introduced into the See of Peter, who are only to be written in the catalogue of Roman Pontiffs to mark such times. For who can say that persons, intruded without law in this way by harlots, can be said to be legitimate Roman Pontiffs? The clergy never elected, nor is there afterwards any consenting mention," &c. Yet succession depends upon this, we are told. Baronius says, "Christ, indeed, seemed to sleep, but he was in the ship; and that this proves the unfailing security of the Church." Of the Church, I believe; not however by, but in spite of, the Popes.

On the death of Lando, Theodora (who lived with Adelbert, Marquis of Tuscany, and whose daughter Marozia was concubine of Pope Sergius), makes John, son of Sergius and Marozia, Pope (John X.). Marozia became wife of Guido, Marquis of Tuscany. She being angry with his brother Peter, had Peter killed, and John seized and put in a dungeon, where he died—they say, suffocated. The Emperor at this epoch got a lance, made out of the nails of Christ's Cross, from Rudolf, King of Burgundy, after threatening fire and sword if he did not give it to him; afterwards gave a large part of Swabia to him, because he gave it up; and always beat his enemies with it.

After Pope Stephen, the Marquis

of Tuscany, and Marozia make another
son of hers, by Pope Sergius, Pope, by
the name of John XI.; but Alberic (son
of Adelbert, Marquis of Tuscany, by
Theodora, not his wife), who ruled at
Rome, put John in prison. There he
remained three years, and there was no
other Pope made. In A.D. 936 Leo VII.
became Pope. I pass over a number
which need no mention. Octavianus, son
of Alberic, was a clergyman; and as he
governed at Rome, made himself Pope
(John), being at the outside not eighteen
years old. Baronius again remarks here
(955, iv.), that though not of an age to be
made bishop, or even deacon, he was
owned afterwards in the succession, the
clergy being supposed to consent, not to
have a schism. The truth is plain enough
—he ruled at Rome. However, the Emperor Otho comes to Rome (A.D. 963), and
holds a council, which deposes John, and
elects Leo VIII., whom Baronius will not

own, because nobody could depose a Pope; yet he was ordained Pope, and ordained priests and deacons, and held the See a year and four months (*Fleury*, book lvi. sec. 7), and they swore fidelity to them. But Otho having sent away some of his troops, the Romans rose against him and tried to kill him; which he knew, and had the advantage; but when the Emperor left, Leo had to fly, and John was Pope again. However, being one night out of Rome with a married woman, he was caught in the act of adultery, and had his head smashed, and died without the sacraments.

The Romans chose Benedict V. Pope. Otho came and besieged them, and they were forced to give up Benedict to him, and Leo re-enters. The Emperor committed Benedict to the keeping of the Archbishop of Hamburg. The Emperor held a council at Rome. Benedict appeared; owned he had sinned; was stripped of his robes, and his pastoral staff broken:

he had joined in deposing John, and swore fidelity to Leo. No wonder Baronius does not own Leo, as he recognized the right of Otho to establish the Pope, of investitures, &c., under pain of excommunication, exile, and death. However, the next Leo was Leo the Ninth, so that on Baronius's principle he must be reckoned such. Baronius has no Leo VIII. at all. After Leo's death they sent to Otho to know whom he would have, and he sent ambassadors to Rome, and John XIII. was chosen. He was followed by Benedict VI. He became odious to the Romans. Crescentius, son of Theodora and Pope John X., took him, shut him up, and afterwards strangled him; while yet alive, Boniface VII. became Pope. After the death of Benedict they drove out Boniface, and Donus became Pope (though some do not count him among the Popes), then a relation of Alberic. But Baronius inserts Donus, but does not count Boniface.

I pass over the Popes named while temporal influence prevailed. The Germans were more respectable; but Baronius does not like them. In A.D. 1002 or A.D. 1003, we have John XVI., called also and commonly XVIII. for a few months, and then John XVII. (usually XIX.) Baronius will not own him but as XVII. because it would be recognizing schismatic Popes. Bar. (x. 1003) puts two Popes John; he says, to make the numbers run right. Crescens had expelled Gregory V. from Rome, and made a Greek Pope. The Emperor and Gregory V. marched together on Rome. But some servants of the Emperor, fearing his clemency (John was a favourite at court), followed, and caught the Pope, and put his eyes out, and put him in prison (*Fleury*, lvii. 50). Benedict VIII. now took the See after Sergius IV., but another party chose Gregory VI. But Benedict, being son of the Count of Tusculum, carried the day; but the party of Gregory VI. roused itself, and Benedict fled to the Emperor. However, Benedict was restored in less than two years.

After Benedict, John, a layman not in orders at all, had the Papacy. He was Benedict's brother, another son of the Count of Tusculum. He got the Papacy, says Fleury, partly by money (lix. 3.), evidently by family influence too. The Patriarch of Constantinople very nearly succeeded in buying the universal Papacy of the East. The Romans drove John XIX. out; but Conrad, the Emperor, came with an army and set him up again: he died that year, A.D. 1033. His nephew, son of Alberic, Count of Tusculum, was made Pope, a boy of about 12 years old, says Fleury; not quite 10, says Glabeus, in Baronius—by money also, and intrigue. (*Fleury*, lix. 81; *Bar.* v. 1033)— Benedict IX. His life was infamous, and through his plunderings and murders

became so odious, that the people drove
him out.   Sylvester III. became Pope,
but only held it three months; he was
of another powerful family, says Baronius.
But Benedict, with the Tusculum family,
attacked Rome, and was reinstated.   But
his conduct became insupportable, and he
agreed to leave for a sum of money, and
the Papal revenue of England, to follow
his pleasures freely; and they made John
Gratian Pope, as Gregory VI.   But all
three called themselves Popes.   Gregory
VI. gave up the Papacy, in a council
called to settle matters, as having entered
on it unlawfully; as Benedict was paid to
go out.   But Baronius, who speaks of it
as a beast with three heads (v. 1044)
coming out of the gates of hell, insists
Gregory VI. was a real Pope, owned so
by Gregory VII., Peter Damianus, &c.
The number designating the Pope is
constantly uncertain, because whether
such or such an one was really Pope is

uncertain. He who is called John XIX.,
Baronius calls XVII. Benedict is VIII.
or IX.; so Stephen.

But when things are at the worst they
mend. The Emperor came, gathered the
clergy and nobles of Rome; they agreed
to have things done decently, and the Emperor took up Suidger, Bishop of Bamberg,
and he became Clement II. No fit person,
it is said, was found in Rome. However,
Clement II. died in nine months, and
Benedict came back and held the Papacy
for nine months. Then, as it seems, repented and gave it up. Sylvester went
back to his See. What came of Gregory
I know not. The Emperor sent Poppo,
Bishop of Brixia, to be Pope. He lived
as Damasus II. twenty-three days, and
was said to be poisoned. Bruno, six
months after, in a diet held at Worms,
was chosen Pope. But Baronius says,
Benedict was tearing it to pieces and
defiling it. So Dupin (xi. century, chap.

iv.), who refers to Clement's being poisoned. A circumstance is to be noted here. Hildebrand, afterwards Gregory VII., came with Bruno. The Romans had sent to the Emperor, and asked him to give them a Pope, through dread, it appears, of Benedict; and after his choice at Worms, Bruno (Leo IX.) came in his pontifical robes. Hildebrand got him to take them off, and be again chosen at Rome. He it was who established the modern Papacy (*Bar.*, *Fleury*, *Dupin*). Everyone who searches for himself must look to the facts, not the title of the Pope, as the succession is so uncertain, that VIII. in one is IX. in the other, and sometimes, as in the Johns, there are three enumerations.

We have seen already the state of the clergy; the buying and sale of benefices was universal, even of the Popedom; and immorality, the most degraded, all but universal among the clergy. The chase and pleasure were their occupation. On the death of Leo, the Romans sent Hildebrand to the Emperor, to choose a Pope in Germany; they had no one fit in Rome. The Emperor assembled a council at Mayence, and Hildebrand got them to choose Gibbard, Bishop of Eichstadt, a near relative to the Emperor, who did not wish to lose him. However, he went, kept his bishopric too, and became Pope. He was very near being poisoned by a subdeacon in the sacrament, but could not lift the cup. They say another devil openly seized the poisoner.

Hildebrand was now the soul of the Papacy at Rome. A great change took place under Nicolas II. On the death of Stephen, the Emperor, who kept things in order, the Roman nobles, the Alberic family, and others, chose the Bishop of Veletri as Pope Benedict. The Cardinals opposed; but Fleury says he held the Papacy nearly ten months; but Hildebrand got the Bishop of Florence chosen at Florence. When he had arrived, the Romans sent to the Emperor, who sanctioned the choice of Florence; the Pope was Nicolas II. He recognized publicly the Emperor's rights, but decreed, when Pope, that the Cardinals should choose the Pope, thus excluding the Emperor and the Roman people. This laid the foundation of the modern Papacy, which was born in Hildebrand, Gregory VII. Therefore it is I have noticed this part of the history. Benedict abdicated.

This was the era of Damianus, whom we have previously cited. Alexander II. was the first chosen by the Cardinals. (A.D. 1061.) Another was chosen at Basle, and consecrated through Lombard influence, Pope Honorius. He came to Rome in arms, was at first victorious, but was afterwards beaten; the German princes deserting him to weaken an infant Emperor. He was deserted by his soldiers, got into the castle of St. Angelo, was besieged two years by Alexander, and then fled. But Honorius never gave up his claim. One great means of the depression of imperial power was, that the Archbishop of Cologne stole away the young Emperor from his mother, who had maintained his authority, and went over to Pope Alexander's side, so that the Emperor was null, though nominally saved. There was a council at Mantua, where the Archbishop appeared, as did Alexander, who was charged also with simony, and Honorius. Alexander was recognized Pope, Honorius pardoned, the Emperor's rights nominally saved, and some of the German party promoted. The Archbishop charged Alexander with having despised the Emperor's rights. P. Damianus wrote on this, that Honorius contrived to claim and exercise Papal authority as far as he could (see *Bar.*, 1064, xl.), and the Archbishop of Ravenna favoured him. After Alexander, Hildebrand was Pope, as Gregory VII. He decreed absolutely the celibacy of the clergy; was resisted everywhere in the north of Europe, where there was some more respect for morality; but prosecuted it earnestly.

The Papal system was now established. I have only to notice, till I come to those near the Reformation, the dying struggles of the imperial power which had given Popes for nearly a century, as Baronius admits, and the Avignon Popes, and the schism; and briefly. Before I turn to this, I give Gregory VII.'s account of the state of the Church. I have not preserved any reference here, but have no doubt of the correctness of the extract. "Alone with my mind's eye, I look at the west, south, and north. I scarcely find Bishops, legally such by their entrance and life, who rule the Christian people for the love of Christ, and not secular ambition; and among all secular princes, I know none who put God's honour before their own, and justice before gain. As to those amongst whom I dwell, as I often tell them, Romans, Lombards, and Normans, I denounce them as, in a certain way, worse than Jews and Pagans."* Gregory having excommunicated the Emperor, the latter and his Bishops chose Guibert (Clement III.) Pope. Gregory would have attacked him at Ravenna with an army. (*Fleury*, iv. 1080.) He sought the help of the Normans, the Italians (Lombardy) and Germany being for the Emperor. The latter (A.D. 1084) entered Rome, set Clement III. on the Papal throne. Gregory retired to St. Angelo. The Emperor besieged him there. Robert

---

* An Abbot Transmundus having put out the eyes of some monks accused of rebellion, and torn out the tongue of one of them, Desiderius, abbot of Casino, put him to penance. Gregory, then cardinal, approved the act, got him out of the abbot's hands, gave him an abbacy, and afterwards made a Bishop of him. Anything for power.

Guiscard, the Norman, freed him, and after staying awhile in Rome, he retired to Salerno, under the protection of the Normans. Gregory VII. died at Salerno. The small Papal party secretly elected Desiderius, Victor III. Clement returned to Rome; he had been expelled A.D. 1089, and came back A.D. 1091 (*Fleury, Bar.*). Didier refused to be Pope, and when chosen went back to Mont Casino, and would not be ordained, but at last yielded. The Normans and others came to Rome, and turned out Clement III. from St. Peter's by force. Still, it appears, he held the upper hand there; for after the death of Victor III. (Didier), Urban, named by him, was chosen at Terracina, under the influence of Mathilde, the great protectress of the Popedom then, by a small assembly, forty persons, clergy and laity, partly by proxy, John, Bishop of Porto, having their authority (*Fleury*, lxiii. 41; *Dupin*, xi. cent. chap. vi.; *Bar.*, i. 1088, *et seq.*)

It is important to notice at this part of the history, that what destroyed the power of Clement and the Emperor in Italy was, that Urban got up the crusades through Peter the hermit, and when that took effect, Clement was rejected. He was driven, it appears, from Rome by the crusaders. Pope Urban, the second (Grat. Decr. Part ii. Caus. xxiii. Quæs. 5, c. 47) says, " Enjoin a measure of suitable satisfaction to those who have killed the excommunicated. For we do not consider those as guilty of homicide who, burning with the zeal of their Catholic mother against the excommunicated, shall have happened to have slain some of them." At this time this was the greater part of Europe.

The remaining facts may be briefly recounted. Pascal II. raised the Emperor's son against him. That son banished him from Rome, and Gregory VIII. was set up as Pope. The Roman

Pope died in exile, or two days after his return; but Gelasius was elected as Roman Pope, but died in exile also soon after. Calistus II. followed as Roman Pope; he treats of peace with the Emperor. Gregory was his prisoner. Calistus was not elected, Baronius admits; he was chosen by a few Cardinals and clergy at Cluny, when Gelasius died, as trusted by him (*Bar.* 1119, i. and v.). After Honorius, there was a contested election between Cardinals and people, but the circumstances are of no moment. After him, the Cardinals who had been beaten in Honorius's case chose Gregory, Innocent II. Other Cardinals and the people chose Peter, Anacletus II., favoured by the laity. Innocent had to leave Rome, went to France, owned by Bernard, and in general in Europe; but Anacletus was Pope at Rome. On Anacletus's death, the schism for the moment is ended by St. Bernard's influence. The Emperor Lothaire brought back Innocent; but as soon as he was gone, Innocent had to go back to Pisa. Gregory was elected in Anacletus's stead as Victor, and submitted to Innocent, but the Romans renounced obedience to the latter. Celestine followed quickly. Baronius says Anacletus's presence at Rome was the triumph of Antichrist, and that it was easy to see who was the successor of St. Peter. (iii. 1130.) The next, Lucius, was killed in a rebellion of the Romans, by a blow of a stone, when assaulting the Capitol; or of chagrin, as some say. Baronius, Dupin, Fleury, do not say how he died. His successor, Eugene, fled from Rome, but returned. Then came Anastasius IV.; Adrian IV. followed. Then a disputed election — Alexander and Victor; the latter given up by the Emperor when beaten by the Lombards. Lucius III. and Urban III. sat at Verona, not at Rome. Lucius fled, being hated and despised by the

Romans, who attacked his territories, and he finally settled at Verona, where Urban was chosen.

From Urban III. on to Boniface VIII., that is, taking in Lucius, from A.D. 1181 to A.D. 1294, the history of the Papacy is that of a worldly power, yet using excommunication as its weapon, contending against the Emperors, using Sicily and Lombardy as their main arms against him with various success, but in result successful. But it wearied the world, and when Boniface attempted to use the acquired power against Philip of France, he signally failed. His successor repeated his acts. And the next Pope, chosen by French influence, removed to Avignon, in France. This, as being practically secular history, I leave untouched. "My kingdom," says the Lord, "is not of this world, else would My servants fight"; the Pope's was.

The most remarkable Pope of the period

was Innocent III., who held the fourth council of Lateran, when transubstantiation was for the first time decreed. He established the inquisition in the crusades against the Albigenses. We may notice that, the See having been vacant three years through election intrigues, there was a compromise, and Gregory X. made a decree for what is now practised, that the Cardinals should be shut up till they chose a Pope. Celestine V. reserved it, and then resigned, as the Cardinals were two years and a half before electing him. The person who got Celestine to resign got himself chosen in his place—it was Boniface VIII. Celestine gives a curious reason to justify his abdication. He says Clement, who was named by Peter, resigned, that no Pope might be named by his predecessor; and then came third after Linus and Anacletus. So Peter made a blunder in beginning the matter. It is known the succession of the first three possessors of the See is hopelessly embroiled.

From A.D. 1309 the Pope lived at Avignon, under French influence and protection, proclaimed his rights over others, and submitted to France. The struggles with the Emperor went on. Louis was set up an anti-Pope at Rome—Nicolas V.; but he was soon given up to his competitor at Avignon. The friar Minorites and Italian Cardinals sided with the Emperor, who was preparing a general council against the Pope, who meanwhile died. Benedict XII. succeeded at Avignon. France would not allow him to make peace with the Emperor; the Emperor was deprived of the sacraments by the Pope; but the clergy who would not administer them were banished. But Louis took ecclesiastical powers in hand, and lost influence. Clement VI. succeeded Benedict, and anathematized the Emperor, and set up an anti-Emperor, who was forced to fly. But the conduct of Clement, who had deposed an ecclesiastical Elector to gain voices for his anti-Emperor, had wearied men of the Popes. Clement got the upper hand, but injured the Papacy. The Electors of the empire meet, and declare the King of Rome receives his power from Electors only.

From A.D. 1313 to A.D. 1316 the See was vacant : the Cardinals would not elect. Clement V., first Pope at Avignon, lived in adultery, sold all the benefices he had to dispose of, and left immense wealth (*Fleury*, 92, xi.). Yet this same Clement, in opening the council of Vienne, describes the state of the whole Church as corruption itself, clergy and laity (*Raynald*, con. of Bar. 1311, lv.). This is Petrarch's account of the court of Avignon. He died in the Papacy of Gregory XI., and had lived at Avignon. " It is the third Babylon, the fifth labyrinth. Here, dreadful prisons, nor the tortuous way of a dark house, nor the fatal mixing of the fate of the human urn ; lastly, not imperious Minos, nor a voracious minotaur, nor the monument of condemned lusts (*veneris*), are wanting; but remedies—love, charity, faith to promises, friendly counsels, or thread by silent help, marking the perplexed way—Ariadne and Dædalus. The only hope of safety is gold! A fierce king is appeased by gold, and heaven is opened by gold; nay more, Christ is sold for gold!"

During this time, from the universal corruption and squeezing for money, the consciences of godly men were rising up against the state of things—Milicz, Matthias Von Jannow, both Bohemians, before Huss; in England, Wickliff (A.D. 1360, &c.). Gregory XI. died at Rome, and a Pope was elected then in a riot: Raynald says the uproar was afterwards. However that may be, for all was violence and confusion, the Cardinals elected another, Clement VII., who went to Avignon; and there were two who divided Europe between them. Benedict XIII. succeeded at Avignon, Boniface IX. at Rome, and then Gregory XII. This brought on the council of Pisa, which put down both. The council chose Alexander V. He dissolves the council, and does not reform.

There were now three Popes. The exaction of money became intolerable, selling of benefices public. It was said it was allowable, as the Pope could not sin in it. This brought on the council of Pisa, "a council," says Bellarmine, "neither manifestly approved nor manifestly condemned" (De Conc. lib. i. c. viii.). That it is approved, the succeeding Alexander being called VI. shews ; for Alexander V. was made Pope by that council, and the same circumstance shews John XXIII. to be confessedly a true Pope, though moderns say no. John XXIII. being obliged to fly, Rome consented to a new council, which met at Constance. Here first they voted by nations. John was deposed, accused of every sort of horrible crime. He had first fled the council. Gregory XII. resigned. Benedict XIII. remained determined, was deposed, and finally deserted by all but the Spanish town he lived in. Martin V. was elected by all. The council had formally decreed a council superior to the Pope, and had acted on it. Martin condemned all appeals from Popes, and after a little reformation dissolved the council. It was here John Huss was burnt, and it was declared that faith was not to be kept with a heretic, he having had letters of safe conduct. Martin confirmed the articles of faith of the council of Constance (*Raynald*, 1418, ii.). Martin V. quarrelled with Cardinals. He appointed a council first at Pavia, then at Siena; but which met afterwards at Basle, under Eugenius. But there was no reformation really, and the universal complaint continued. France made regulations for herself. Eugene IV. succeeded Martin V.

The iniquities with which John XXIII. was charged were so dreadful, that when presented to the chief men of the council of Constance they thought it better not to have him called to account—the Apostolic See would be discredited altogether, and all his promotions of ecclesiastics held void.

I should add, that the council of Constance had ordered that a council should be held within a limited time, and a second within seven years, and these were held in consequence. Eugenius, fearing reformation from the first, sought to dissolve the council. The council, under his own legate, resisted, confirmed the decrees of Constance that a council was above the Pope, and could decide so as to subject all, the Pope included, in articles of faith, schism, and reformation. The cry was universal, in these councils, for reformation in head and members. The French held a national council to back up the council of Basle against the Pope's effort, and even the Emperor, though yielding to the Pope for a time to get crowned, returned to the council. But this Pope tried it out. It condemned the Pope, and deposed him, and elected Felix V. Meanwhile, the council having cited the Pope. (A.D. 1437) to appear before it, he appointed a council at Ferrara, and the two sat together. The council of Ferrara condemns that of Basle. From Ferrara it was transferred to Florence. The council of Florence ended in A.D. 1442. The Pope appointing one in Rome; that at Basle, in A.D. 1444, appointing one in Germany. Felix V. had one at Lausanne. But subsequently resigned the Papacy, on condition of having all his Cardinals and promotions to benefices owned, and certain personal privileges. Nicolas, the other Pope, withdrew all his acts against him and the council of Basle.

The Pope of Rome had thus seemingly

gained uncontested supremacy; but the fact that all the respectable clergy had met, condemned deposed Popes, and named others whose successors all subsequent Popes have been, made their position very different. All their theologians avoid, if possible, pronouncing a judgment on these councils, even when they hold the supremacy of the Pope in the highest way. Bellarmine admits that Pisa can neither be approved nor condemned. If it be condemned, the Pope is not Pope, for the Popes are the successors of the council's nominee; if it be approved, then a council can depose a Pope. Neither proposition would do. The like is the case of Constance. That council deposed three Popes, and chose another. But, then, it openly declared that a Pope was subject to a general council, and that a council represented the universal Church, and could act in its name, and was infallible; and it acted on it; and again, the succession depends on their act. Moreover, Martin V. sanctioned the doctrine that a general council represents the whole Church (*Fleury*, 106, xiv.). Bellarmine recognizes the power of a council to settle schism. He refers to Popes Cornelius, Symmachus, Innocent II., Alexander III., and the Pisa and Constance councils. No remedy, he says, is more powerful than a council. So for false doctrines in Popes, as Marcellinus, Damasus, Sixtus III., Leo III. and IV. Marcellinus, he says, had to confess it; the rest purged themselves.

Now, though the Popes had the upper hand, the universal conscience of the Church was roused; the weightiest, godliest doctors declared there must be reform in the head and in the members. This became the universal cry all over Europe; whenever the Pope went too far, there was an appeal to a general council. France maintained, in what are called the Gallican liberties, the doctrine of Constance. The Popes themselves (instead of governing an ignorant and prostrate Europe, whose princes, being divided and jealous of one another, were glad of the Pope's help, while he was always himself and one in his purpose, and scrupled at no weapons), were now judged by laity and clergy, who were subject to them, and gave themselves up to mere petty local ambition. France and Germany were considerably emancipated in the spirit of men's minds, deliverance being looked for anxiously, and though disappointed in their hopes of redress from the councils, were groaning so much the more, though hopelessly, under the burden. Spain and Portugal were more content, because they liked that title of the Pope which divided the new world between them. But men's spirits craved deliverance; threatened councils, appealed to them, were ripe for some deliverance. The unheard of infamies of Alexander VI., and even the crimes and conduct of Sixtus and Julius, only sunk the Papacy lower, though none opposed it; and the shameless sale of indulgences, practically an allowance to sin, gave the last blow to man's conscience, and opened the door to the testimony of an offended God. I shall briefly trace this, which will lead us to the Reformation.

Nicolas V. arranged matters peaceably with Felix V., the Lausanne Pope, who was during his life to be respected as such, though without power. Calixtus IV. followed him. They succeeded in gaining influence in Germany; but the attempt to rouse the people to a crusade against the Turks utterly failed. Pius II. failed in like attempts; he condemned appeals to a general council (*Raynald*, 1460, x. xi.), where we see it was become a general thing. This same Pope, as Æneas Sylvius, had been a great adherent of the council of Basle. Paul II. was arbitrary. The cardinals at this time bound themselves all when in conclave, as in the case of Eugenius, to reform the Papal court in head and members, hold a council, and to many other points. Eugene confirmed this by a bull. Paul bound himself in the same way, but by a decree rejected it all, and by cajoling and violence forced all the Cardinals but one to join him, though some very reluctantly (*Raynald*, 1431, v., 1458, v., 1464, lxi. lxii.). Platina complains bitterly of his undoing iniquitously all Pius II. had done, threatened to complain to kings and princes (for parliaments, universities, kings, everybody did so now), and have a general council, and got put in prison and in the stocks for his pains.

Sixtus IV. succeeded. He occupied himself with low Italian intrigues and conspiracy to advance his family. Innocent VIII. came after him. He was famous for promoting and enriching his illegitimate children, though one of the conditions (in conclave) of election was not to do it. He was the subject of pasquinades on this account. Rome, they said, might well call him father. It appears he had seven children while Pope. The general fact is stated by Raynald (1492, xxiii.). He received pay from the Sultan for keeping a rival brother safe when the Turks were invading Europe.

To Alexander VI. one hardly knows how to refer. He is recognized to have been—except it be his own second illegitimate son—the most horrible fiend who has come under public notice. A thorough debauchee at all times, so as to attract notice and reproof even at the Papal court. Elected Pope by bribery and promises, he got rid in one way or another of those who promoted him. His second son killed his eldest brother, and the Pope's other favourite, Peroto, who had hidden himself in the Pope's mantle, so that the blood spurted up in the Pope's face (Casillo, Appendix to Ranke). Alexander had made a Cardinal of him when quite young, but he left the clerical order to be a prince in Italy. France made him Duke of Valentinois, to reward the Pope for his divorce. He killed his sister's husband to marry her better. This same sister, when the Pope was away, kept the Papal court, and opened the despatches, consulting the Cardinals. She was one of the Pope's five illegitimate children. Her marriage was celebrated with pomp in the Pope's palace. Infessina's language is bitter to a degree on the occasion, and he declares that the universal corruption of the clergy through Innocent and Alexander's care of their children made men fear it might reach the monks and people of religion. " Although," he adds, " the monasteries of the city were almost all (*quasi omnia*) turned into brothels, no one gainsaying it." The current lines on him were, " Alexander sells kings, altars, Christ. He first bought them, he has a good right to sell them." Engaged with his second son Borgia in poisoning (as he had poisoned others already) some rich Cardinals, to get their money, at a feast prepared for it, he took, being very hot, the poisoned wine and died.

I cannot be expected to go into the details of such a life as this. Raynald tries to cover the way he met his death, but no one believes him. The very brief pontificate of Pius III. needs no notice. Julius II. was engaged in wars. The Cardinals had all sworn to reform, and have a general council. He was occupied fighting against the Venetians, and after-wards the French, &c. Louis XII. had a council at Tours. Germany prepared her griefs, and sought a pragmatic sanction like France. The French council held that the King could renounce allegiance to the Pope.   He should keep the decrees of Basle, and appeal to a future council. If Julius armed, pronounced sentence upon him or his allies, it would be of no force whatever.   The King and Emperor summoned a general council at Pisa, but it was mainly composed of French Bishops.   The Pope convoked another at the Lateran.   The Pisan came to nothing, though it deposed the Pope by a decree. A number of Cardinals were engaged in it, founded on Julius' promise to have a general council within two years.   I only refer to it to show the confusion all was in.   The Emperor and King of France adhered afterwards to the Lateran. Francis I. and Leo X. made a treaty. The Pope by this had again quietly the upper hand.   The councils of Constance and Basle, on the first of which the succession of the Papacy depends, maintained the authority of councils and

Bishops.   France held strongly to this. The councils of Florence and Lateran V. set up the Pope.   In result half Europe broke off, and the Pope by the council of Trent remained absolute in the rest, if we except the Gallican liberties.

This brings us to the last act which brought about the Reformation: not the wisdom of princes, nor the power of councils, but God rousing conscience and faith—conscience long wearied, and faith which He gave, roused by the excessive wickedness which the Popes, grown secure in wickedness, countenanced for mere esthetical purposes.   Julius II. had begun St. Peter's, Leo wanted to finish it.   Italy had been flooded with fresh light from Constantinople, and the educated clergy were infidels.   Elegant Latin or Greek alone was sought after, pleasure and literary pursuits.   It is said that Leo himself was an infidel; but there is no proof of it.   At any rate, St. Peter's was to be finished, and for this purpose money was to be raised. For this purpose an old expedient, by which the piety of the ignorant had been before that imposed on, was resorted to, but with a recklessness which passed all bounds. Indulgences were issued, as to which there are very pretty theories, but which are nothing less than allowances to commit sin for money. I know well it is said to be commutation of penance, and shortening consequently the duration of purgatorial pains; but penance had taken place of the need of holiness, and as a man with the sacraments would not go to hell, purgatory had taken the place of hell, and when a man wanted to sin, he got rid of the purgatory he was afraid of by paying a sum of money: he wanted to sin, and paid so much money to do it with impunity. Guilt (*culpa*) was settled by sacraments, so that he did not much trouble himself about it; the pains which remained, about which he did care, by

money. Now, too, it was not provided
for troubled sinners, but offered everywhere to bold ones who wanted to sin.
Each sin had its price. The object was
to get money. Grace, or holiness, or
any doctrine, no matter which, was not
thought of.

Albert, brother of Joachim, of Branden-
burg—a young, elegant, sumptuous Archbishop of Mayence, and Elector, spent,
like Leo, more than he could afford,
and applied to Leo for the farming of
the indulgences; but he had not paid
for his pallium, or archiepiscopal robe,
some 30,000 florins, and could not have
it without; for the Pope wanted money,
and Cardinal Pucci had suggested this
means of getting it. The Fuggers were
bankers of Augsburg, and Albert owed
them money already; however, the affair
seemed a good one, and they advanced
the money for the pallium, and became
bankers for the indulgence-money. A

certain Tetzel, whose life, it is said, the Elector of Saxony had already saved, when Maximilian was going to put him in a sack and throw him into the Inn, and who had before preached indulgences with success, undertook the matter for Albert. It is stated that he declared, that if a person had violated the Virgin Mary, he could give him pardon: that as soon as the money was in the box, the souls were out of purgatory. It is certain, from his own statement, that he urged that when a man had pardon (plenary remission, says the instruction) for his sins on confession and contrition, which he got on confessing them, or undertaking to do it, still for mortal sin there was seven years' penance on earth; and men committed countless ones, and God knew how long they would be in purgatory; and that, save for four cases, reserved to the Pope, he could give pardon for everything now, at any time on confession,* and plenary at the hour of death, so that they would slip purgatory altogether for a small sum. As to condemnation, the confession, contrition, and absolution had put all that out of the question.

The Jesuit Maimbourg does not attempt to conceal the iniquity of what was and had been going on. Before this, indulgences had been largely used to make money—farmed out to quæstors, who made all the money of them they could. It was one of the charges against John XXIII., giving power to his Legate to appoint confessors, and free every one from sins, and all the penalty besides, if they paid what they were rated at. Still, Maimbourg admits it went on with Leo all the same, that Tetzel was employed because he had

* The instructions themselves to Tetzel are in Gerdes' Hist., Ev. Ren. vol. i., document ix. These say once in life, and in the hour of death even, for reserved cases; for others as often as need was. Sec. 30.

got in great sums for the Teutonic knights, that the agents made people believe they were sure of their salvation, and souls were delivered out of purgatory as soon as the money was paid; and as they saw the clerks of these same agents carousing in taverns on their profits, much indignation was created (Maimbourg's *History of Lutheranism*, 3rd edition, 12mo, Paris, p. 9 *et seq.*).   This, he admits, was the origin of Protestantism.   No doubt Popes had made money of indulgences before. It was now an habitual resource; that is, religious iniquity of the profoundest kind was.   The sale of liberty to sin was the settled practice of the Roman Church; the authorised practice and doctrine of its Popes and leaders.   It was farmed out to profit.   I repeat, no heathenism, horrible as was its corruption, ever was guilty of such deep and dark iniquity.

It will be said that Tetzel's conduct was a gross abuse.   Be it so.   To a rightly-

constituted mind, the principle is far worse
than the abuse. The Pope, getting money
to build or ornament a grand church, by a
universal commutation of godly discipline
(if we go no farther) for money, really for
an allowance of all sorts of sin for money,
is worse than the abuses that a reckless
agent may be guilty of.   Dr. N. knew
this ; an ignorant man might be ignorant
of this.   Dr. N. was not ; he knew this
gave birth to Protestanism.   Has he not
learned to hate such things as this ?

In Leo's time light had come in ; the
condemning of Popes by councils had
weakened confidence ; the people were
weary of the iniquity long ago, but the
authority that sanctioned it had now lost
a great deal of its influence, and the
excessive insult to conscience, shewn in
the present sale of indulgences, filled the
cup.   The princes were angry at their
oppression by the Pope ; they had long
complained, though they had not dared

to stir.   But when God raised up Luther to apply the Word of God to the conscience, and shew the iniquity of all this, and after some time the want of foundation for the Pope's power, all was providentially prepared.   People came to confess to him, guilty of all sorts of crimes; and when he insisted on putting practical penance on them, they produced their letters of indulgence, and were easy in their sin.   My business here is not to pursue the history of the Reformation. For my own part, I do not for a moment think it established the Church on its original basis; nor did its leaders see that any more than Dr. Newman does; but it was the righteous rising up of faith, with the power of the truth and Word of God, as far as it was possessed, against the most iniquitous system that ever the sun looked on, which nations and conscience were alike weary of.   I challenge Dr. Newman, or any one else,

to shew me a like system of iniquity
in the world. That gave rise to Protestantism. If natural conscience, even,
was not to have been finally destroyed by
the heads and authorities of Christendom,
it must have protested. That protest
first made by Luther's faith was Protestantism.

I have followed out the historical state
of what Dr. N. looks at as the holy
Catholic Church, and that of the Popes
its leaders, according to him, the alleged
vicegerents of Christ on earth. If details
were gone into, and the statements of
private historians, all would appear far
darker than I have made it. But it is
needless. A righteous soul will judge
whether "the note" of holiness is to be
found in this history. That upright souls
there were who groaned under it, I admit.
But what did they groan under? Who
made them groan?

But Dr. N. tells us that normal infallibility resides in a Pope and general council. "It is to the Pope in œcumenical council that we look as to the normal seat of Infallibility" (p. 256). I will therefore run through the œcumenical councils, and see what we can trust to in them.

Constantine, the first Christian Emperor, meddled, as did his successors, largely in ecclesiastical matters. As a political man, he felt his government hindered by the dissensions of the Bishops, which roused the whole Christian world. He took up the Donatist question; he directed certain Bishops to hear the same a second time, others to rehear it, and at last heard it himself, and put the Donatists down. Meanwhile, the Arian controversy raged in the East. It had spread from Alexandria over the whole eastern world, and divided the people into two factions (Euseb. *Life of Const.*, book ii. 61 to the end). Thereupon the Emperor writes a letter, saying the East had been the source of light to the world; how grieved he was, and so on, that, as they were one in faith (Alexander and Arius), they ought to hold their tongues on nice points, and not let such delicate questions come before the ignorant, and make confusion. But in vain; so he summoned a council at Nice in the hope of settling it. The invitations came from himself, and he provided horses for the Bishops to come, or allowed them to use the public posts; he had them to meet in the palace, and presided himself. A glowing description is given by Eusebius of his coming into the assembly, and taking his seat at the head of it. When the Bishops had bowed, and said a few complimentary words, he sat down, and the Bishops too. Then he made a long harangue to them, and gave liberty of speech afterwards to the Bishops, soothed them, answered objections, reasoned with them, and brought them, though with difficulty, to some kind of quietness, and got all but five to sign, who were banished.

The Emperor held thus a strong hand over them; having once made a decision in a council, little or big, he enforced it for peace' sake by his own authority. The orthodox suffered as others, if they were not quiet: Athanasius himself among the rest. That Constantine convoked and managed the council is beyond all question; Eusebius, Ruffinus, Epiphanius all agree; that he presided is equally certain; he sat in a little golden seat at the head, the Bishops down the sides of the apartment. Alexander of Alexandria, Epiphanius tells us, got him to convoke it. Hosius subscribed first, then the two presbyters sent by Silvester of Rome, then the rest.

I may note here, that in the early councils scarce any Western Bishops were ever present. The West had not the mental activity of the East, and they did not raise useless questions as the Easterns did.   In no one of the first six general councils were there a dozen Western Bishops, in many not half that number. Three are found in this first one.   A note, said to be of Dionysius Exiguus, says, they did not sign at Nice, because they were not suspected of heresy (Hard. i. 311). If this were so, it gives a curious character to the decrees and signatures.   It was to force the suspected Bishops to declare and bind themselves.   The number of prelates is uncertain; Eusebius says 250.   In Hardouin you have 318 names, which afterwards was held to be a mystical number.

The late councils were, on the contrary, wholly Western, and of the Latin Church. There were no Easterns.   At Florence Pope Eugenius attempted it, but it was a complete failure; the assent a few Greek prelates did give was utterly repudiated by their Church when they went home.   All these late Western councils, save Pisa, Constance, and Basle, were assemblies called and managed by the Popes for their own purposes, with in general a vast majority of Italian Bishops. Pisa, Constance, and Basle were the fruit of the struggles of the conscience of Christendom against the hopeless wickedness and oppression of the Papacy and the Popes. There has been no council since which represented East and West. It was attempted at Sardica, and failed; they split, and held two; the most complete one was Ariminium, under Constantius, where 400 Bishops undid the work of Nice by dropping the words—"of one substance with the Father," though they rejected many statements of Arius: but it did not succeed; the Westerns had been dragged in, and afterwards protested. Catholicity is a fable as to fact. As to holiness, to seek it leads into a tissue of horrible facts. Unity in the outward body there has been none, since the

pretensions of the Popes and Constantinople began.

The second so-called general council
consisted of 150 Eastern Bishops, called
together by Theodosius ; and the Bishops
so declare in their letter which precedes
the decrees, and ask expressly the confirmation by the Emperor of what they had
decreed. They communicate their decrees
and canons to the Western Bishops in
common, then assembled at Rome, giving
Constantinople the second rank after Rome,
but on grounds which refer merely to civil
rank in each. They confirm the sixth
canon of the council of Nice as to the
independence of the larger divisions of
the hierarchical system. Their creed is
the now accepted Nicene one, an article
forbidden by Pope Leo being added. But
the Pope had nothing to say to the council;
the Popes did not accept its canons ; but
they are received in the universal Church.
Baronius seeks to invalidate one, but is

corrected by Pagi, who shews it to have been universally received.

It is worthy of note here, that the article added to their creed is still rejected by the Greeks, who hold the creed as settled by the council of Constantinople. And it is further to be remarked, that the general council of Ephesus forbade any other creed to be proposed to any one, and the great Pope Leo, the means of Dr. N.'s becoming a Romanist, this very article in particular. This added article, which came from Spain and France, is the great subject of division with the Greeks, though they do not believe in purgatory either, nor, of course, recognize the Popes. Not only did Pope Leo formally forbid its being inserted, but had the Constantinopolitan creed engraved in Greek and Latin on silver plates on this account in the Church (Comp. Pearson on the Creed, on the eighth article, where the authorities are cited).

We have not much security from

councils as yet, nor is the Pope found in an œcumenical council hitherto, save by his presbyters at Nice, who subscribed in their place after Hosius, the Emperor's confidant, as it appears. The council of Ephesus followed, in which the Pope acted very ably by his Legates, but in which no other Western prelates were present. The Emperor had convoked the council, and his commissioner forbade them to meet till all the Eastern prelates were there; but Cyril, and the Bishops of his party, drove him out, took possession of all the churches, and settled the matter by condemning Nestorius before the Easterns came, Nestorius and his party protesting, but not daring to go. The Easterns, however, did not yield; Cyril was excommunicated and deposed by them; and it was only on Cyril's giving up some points, that John of Antioch was reconciled some years later to Cyril, through the Emperor's means. The result was, Nestorianism spread through the East even to China. The Emperor gave up Nestorius to have peace, and he was banished. But Leo, in his letter subsequently to Flavian of Constantinople, adopted at the council of Chalcedon, does not use the word Nestorius objected to — *Deipara*. The whole course of Cyril was a disgrace to any sober Christian man; he was the true source of Eutychianism, and I judge his soundness very questionable on the atonement.

The next council of Ephesus was convoked, as the previous one; the Pope's representatives were in it. But Cyril's violence against Nestorius had left Eutychian sects at Alexandria, and bore its fruits here. The Archbishop of Alexandria presided as before. Why was not the Holy Ghost here? Yet they beat the poor old Archbishop of Constantinople in such a way, that he died of it in a few days, and others were sorely maltreated.

Pope Leo condemned Eutyches in the famous epistle to Flavian, too rhetorical for such a subject, and questionable, I judge, in some expressions; but doubtless a remarkable document, and substantially sound, and asked for a council in or near Italy. The Emperor refused; but the council—first convened at Nice, and then removed to Chalcedon—was held, which also condemned Eutyches, adopting Leo's statement and Cyril's two letters to Nestorius, on the ground of their intrinsic merits. The Legates asked if this and the other councils agree with Leo. The Bishops answered, Leo agrees with them. There was a great struggle for jurisdiction and rank between Leo and Anatolius, the Legates having orders to resist all advance in rank of Constantinople. Leo's predecessor denied any to it. But it was maintained and increased to equal dignity and second rank in precedence, and the contested jurisdiction given it, the Legates staying away that day, then complaining of its being done; but it was confirmed. Anatolius gave way afterwards in form, but kept his ground in fact. The canon remains in the universal canons; but the Popes would never own it. Pretty work for the lowly servants of Christ! The Romans were charged with forging part of a canon here to give supremacy to Rome, as they were convicted of it just at this time in Africa, which peremptorily rejected the pretensions of Rome, and sent off its Legate. But what I mainly refer to in the council was this, that Theodore and Ibas were declared sound in the faith. And Leo confirmed twice over the doctrinal decisions of the council. But in the following œcumenical council, Pope Vigilius first gave a judgment in favour of the three chapters, as it was called; but he had to do with a powerful Emperor who had now re-conquered Italy, and he made the Pope come to the council, and finally forced

him * to sign and confirm its decrees,
which condemned the three chapters
which Chalcedon had pronounced sound,
by which confirmation, moreover, Baronius
says it became a general council. But if
it did, we have alleged infallible authority,
a Pope in an œcumenical council, condemning what the same infallibility
approves. What kind of infallibility or
security is this? The truth is, the best of
these councils were disgraceful scenes of
turbulent violence, even Chalcedon.

God has taken care of His Church and
the faith, that is true, blessed be His
name; and He uses any means He
pleases; but the history of the means
shows, that if they are rested in, it is
worse than a broken reed. It is an
utterly false principle to sanction the
means God has employed, because He
has employed them. The wickedness of

* I do not enter into the details: they were wretched
enough.

the Jews was the means God employed for our salvation, with the utter want of conscience of Pilate. Who justifies them ?

The third general council was perfectly shameful, and really produced lasting disasters to the Church at large. No one acquainted with history can deny it. It was really the fruit of the Pope's jealousy of Constantinople, and consequent intrigues. Constantinople had not been what was called an apostolic See; was raised to eminence by the importance of the city as the capital. Old Rome could not bear this. At any rate, these councils, which we are told are to secure us, rested the pre-eminence of Rome and Constantinople on their being capitals, old and new Rome. The Christian has nothing to do with these worldly intrigues. They enable him to judge the whole system by the faith of Him whose kingdom was not of this world. At any rate, general councils confirmed by Popes have directly contradicted one another. In very deed, if we examine their history, we find no trace of the Spirit's presence, but every proof of His absence, though the faith may have been substantially preserved.

I am not writing a history of the Councils, but meeting what is referred to in Dr. N.'s self-defence. I pass to three others, to show how groundless, how wild these foundations of faith are; how unsimple, compared with the precious Word of God, the statements of the Lord and His inspired Apostles, or other servants.

First, Pisa. Here is a council on which the whole succession of the Pope and Roman clergy depends. Yet Bellarmine declares that it is a council which can neither be approved nor condemned. The reason is very simple; there were two Popes, Benedict and Gregory. The council was formed by a number of cardinals of each, and the prelates and others they brought together. They summoned formally the two Popes, and deposed them; chose a third, who confirmed all their acts, and is recognized Pope. If they do accept the council, then it is above the Pope, and can act without him; for this is what amongst other things is confirmed. If they do not accept it, then the succession of Popes is a false one. Benedict and Gregory held their ground, but in vain. The council had decreed a new council, and Alexander, the newly elected Pope, had John for his successor. The Emperor was able to get him to hold a council, to which he went. Here was normal infallibility; but the council deposed him for crimes, and the other two as schismatics, &c., and chose a fourth, Martin, whose authority, of course, depended on that of the council. He tried to destroy it by an evasive confirmation, and closed it without any reforms.   Now, if normal infallibility rests in a Pope in œcumenical council, it is not to be found at all; for in the early councils they contradicted one another, to say nothing of their being horrible bear gardens; and in the later ones, the existence of Popes depends on their action without a Pope amongst them.

Is it to this the Christian is reduced—he who seeks the truth, or even the true Church?   He cannot receive a priest, nay, not a sacrament, till he knows he is one. I say this on their own ground, and we are supposing a person inquiring.   He cannot take it for granted, or he is decided already;   he looks to the person who established the priest, and finally to the ultimate source of certainty and authority. In Rome it cannot be found.   It is not a question of profiting by a recognized ministry, but finding the truth, and a true one.   But this normal seat of infallibility is not to be found by a person competent to inquire; and what a thing to search for, when their own authorities cannot tell me which council, or what part of it, has authority, if a person is not competent!

Whereas, if I receive the Scriptures as the word of God (and if not, I am an infidel), I have the teaching of Paul, and Peter, and John, and of the blessed Lord Himself. Surely I have need of holiness and grace to learn; but I have infallible authority to learn from. It is in vain to say it is a rule of faith, not a proper means of communicating truth. I insist urgently on the difference. I may learn there; I may have learnt from my mother, a minister, or others. I may have done so from the Bible. But I have a certain rule there; the Romanist has none, if the question is raised. They say the universal Church is right. But where is it to be found? The majority of Christians, and the most ancient churches, are outside Rome. One will tell me the seat of this

authority is in the Pope; another, the Pope
with a council; another, a council as independent of and above a Pope. And if
this last be not held, there is no true Pope
to be had, no true succession. And this
not as an individual argument; it has
been decreed twice, by assembled Christendom, held by universities the most
famous in the world, denounced, no doubt,
the other side of the Alps, at Rome. But
when I enquire of their greatest authority
about that council, on which their cause
depends, which was confirmed absolutely
by a Pope, I am told it is uncertain—
cannot be condemned or approved! As
another is a secret not to be spoken of!
There is no known seat of infallibility for
a person capable of inquiring. The whole
thing is as foreign from God's dealings, and
His way of securing us in the truth, as it
is possible to be. I might much enlarge
upon this point, but I refrain. What I
have said is enough to show what the

Roman Church system produced, as its own best authors record it (individual authors teem with reproaches and scorn), what its Popes were, what refuge its councils were to the inquiring mind. I close this part of my inquiry.

The question of Dr. Newman's honesty has been raised. It is a painful kind of subject. But, I must say, I don't think him honest. I don't in the least mean that gross dishonesty which sets about to deceive and say what is false. But a false way always begets false ways—that kind of dishonesty of which Scripture says, " Deceiving and being deceived." Every one saw, and Monsignore Wiseman saw, as he tells us, and Dr. Newman knew, that his path led to Rome. He counted Rome the most exalted Church in the world; hated Protestantism; thought he had a special mission to reform Anglicanism; had a presentiment that he himself should land in Popery; admits now the scope and issue of the movement was such; knew his leading was leading others into it; hence, was willing to bend the stick beyond what was straight, in order to straighten it—that is, to go beyond the truth to gain the result he wished. He was not, as many thought that he was, a concealed Romanist, seeking to gain others; but he did know or feel where it led, though there were difficulties from habits of thought in his own mind, yet continued without his conscience being stirred as to the path he was pursuing, and bending every thing, as, I must say, no honest mind could do, to the purpose he had in view. I suppose, from what he says of visions and secret feelings as to a mission, that there was some direct action of Satan : else it was connected with the most absolute confidence in himself, and the most total absence of the truth, or any concern in it. When he joined Romanism, he did not yet believe its principal tenets;

he submitted to authority—that authority, I have no doubt, Satan's. It is characteristic of Rome to be regardless of the truth, of Christ to be the truth. It is the more solemn in his case, because he declares he is now certain that he was converted to God by that which he gave up.

Till the end of 1842 he was in doubt, not certain that Rome was right. But long before this, for he *disclosed* it in 1839, he had a strong presentiment that his existing opinions would ultimately give way, and that the grounds of them were unsound. Only before 1839 he felt such a strong presentiment was not a sufficient ground for disclosing the state of his mind (p. 215). Perhaps not, if he had not been active in a work and mission confided to him. At that time he knew (p. 133) he was disposing young men's minds towards Rome. This in 1839, and he had mentioned his general difficulty to A. B. a year before. He stayed then, because he had not made trial how much the English Church would bear. "As to the result," he says "viz., whether this process will not approximate the whole English Church, as a body, to Rome, that is nothing to us" (p. 135). I am more certain that the Protestant spirit which I oppose leads to infidelity, than that which I recommend leads to Rome. In p. 156 we read, "I have felt all along that Bishop Bull's theology was the only theology on which the English Church could stand. I have felt that opposition to the Church of Rome was *part* of that theology, and that he who could not protest against the Church of Rome was no true divine in the English Church. I have never said, nor attempted to say, that any one in office in the English Church, whether Bishop or incumbent, could be otherwise than in hostility to the Church of Rome." Yet in the next page he says, "You cannot tell how sad your account of Moberly has made me. His view of the sinfulness of the decrees of Trent is as much against union of churches as against individual conversions." In p. 71 he tells us, "We had a real wish to co-operate with Rome in all lawful things, if she would let us, and if the rules of our Church let us; and we thought there was no better way towards the restoration of doctrinal purity and unity." Yet opposition to the Church of Rome was part of the theology of the Church of England divines, and none in office in the Church of England could be otherwise than in hostility to the Church of Rome, yet he talks of saving his protest.

So as regards the Articles. "I wished to institute an enquiry how far in critical fairness the text *could* be opened. I was aiming far more at ascertaining what a man who subscribed it might hold, than what he must, so that my conclusions

were negative rather than positive." (p. 80.)
" In addition, I was embarrassed in consequence of my wish to go as far as
possible in interpreting the Articles in the
direction of Roman dogma, without disclosing what I was doing to the parties
whose doubts I was meeting, who . . .
might be thereby encouraged to proceed
still farther than at present they found in
themselves any call to go." This, he tells
us, was from being enjoined, he thinks,
by his Bishop to keep the men straight
who were going into Popery through his
means.

What a labyrinth of disingenuousness!
I ask any man if this be plain uprightness?
I do not mean he intended to deceive;
but a false way, I repeat, leads to false
ways. His pretension to reform the
Anglican system, for which he had had
a vision and a charge, led him into this
tortuous course, through absolute confidence in himself. My reader will perhaps

s

say that it is a hard word, "absolute confidence in himself." It is his own. In
the storm that arose on Tract 90 he says,
" But how was I any more to have absolute confidence in myself ? how was I
to have confidence in my present confidence ?" (p. 89.) Am I wrong in saying,
a vision, a mission, a charge ? (p. 32.)
Going abroad he wrote the verses about
his guardian angel, which begin with
these words—

" Are these the tracks of some unearthly friend ?"

and goes on to speak of " the vision
which haunted me." While abroad he
repeated to himself the words, even of
old dear to him, " *Exoriari aliquis.* . . . . .
I began to think I had a mission " (p. 34),
and so wrote to his friends. It was at
this time he said, " We have a work to
do in England." Nor did this ever leave
him. When Tract 90 came out, in writing
to Dr. Bagot, of the See of Oxford, he

says (p. 91), " I think I can bear, or at least will try to bear, any personal humiliation, so that I am preserved from betraying sacred interests which the Lord of grace and power has given into my charge." The words of St. Augustine, *Securus judicat orbis terrarum*—the whole world judges in security—came into his mind as a light from heaven, in connection with Leo and the monophysites, and Cardinal Wiseman's lecturing on the Anglican claim. " I had seen the shadow of a hand upon the wall. . . . . The heavens had opened and closed again." (p. 118.) At this time he wrote the sermon in which it is said, " Compared with this one aim, of not being disobedient to a heavenly vision." Now, what was this mission? At this time the effect of the vision was, " the Church of Rome will be found right after all." Already, when abroad, we have seen he held Rome to be the most exalted of all Churches. In

1839 he held the Churches of Rome and England were both one. His *via media* was then gone (p. 120). His mission was to reform the Anglican Church.

But in the beginning of 1839, in an article in the *British Critic*, he says (p. 101), " Lastly, I proceeded to the question of that future of the Anglican Church which was to be a new birth of the ancient religion." Yet he had no prospect as to it ; the age was moving towards Rome, he knew (p. 167). But, in defending Anglicanism, he did not at all mind framing a sort of defence which they (the High Church clergy) "might call a revolution, while I thought it a restoration. Thus, for illustration, I might discourse upon the communion of saints in such a manner (though I do not recollect doing so) as might lead the way towards devotion to the blessed Virgin and the saints on the one hand, and towards prayers for the dead on the other." " If

the Church be not defended on establishment grounds, it must be upon principles
which go far beyond their immediate
object. Sometimes I saw these further
results, sometimes not. Though I saw
them, I sometimes did not say that I saw
them. . . . It was indeed one of my great
difficulties and causes of reserve, as time
went on, that I at length recognized, in
principles which I had honestly preached
as if Anglican, conclusions favourable to
the cause of Rome. Of course, I did
not like to confess this; and, when in-
terrogated, was in perplexity. St. Leo
had overset, in my own judgment, its
(antiquity's) force in the special argument
for Anglicanism, yet I was committed to
antiquity, together with the whole Anglican school. What, then, was I to say
when acute minds urged this or that
application of it against the *via media?*
It was impossible that, in such circumstances, any answer could be given which

was not unsatisfactory, or any behaviour adopted which was not mysterious." Now this was already the case in 1839 (p. 168). He was preaching principles favourable to the Roman Church at that date; knowing them to be such, did not confess it, and was mysterious in his conduct.

Is it possible that Dr. N. now does not see the want of simplicity and uprightness in this? When he found out he was preaching principles favourable to Rome, when he declares a true Anglican divine must be hostile; if he could not bring himself to confess it, could he not have stopped, instead of *adopting* a mysterious behaviour? I certainly judge an honest man would have done so. He says in this page, "I simply deny that I ever said anything which secretly bore against the Church of England, knowing it myself, in order that others might unwarily accept it." But for him, as we have seen, the whole question was between the Churches of England and Rome. He recognized, by 1839 at any rate, that he was, in effect, preaching in favour of the latter. When he continued to do so, was it that others might accept it or not? He was all this time remaining without any satisfactory basis for a religious profession, in a state of moral sickness, neither able to acquiesce in Anglicanism, nor able to go to Rome. "But I bore it, till in course of time my way was made clear to me" (p. 66). But he had the presentiment he was going there, was teaching conclusions favourable to it, knew it, and preached on, and was mysterious in behaviour, with the conviction that he had a mission from some heavenly vision, to which he would not be disobedient—that vision being that Rome was right. He had a secret longing love of Rome (p. 165) preached conclusions favourable to Rome, knew it, but never said anything which secretly bore against the Church of England.

Dr. N. may think this honest; I avow I cannot. His friends may attribute it more to his "absolute confidence in myself." This, doubtless, had a share in it. But it does not make it honest. He had a great sense of his own importance. His secession is "a great act" (p. 169). It is a great event. But this does not solve this question of honesty. He was seeking disciples (p. 217) till he gave up his place in the movement; but this last was only after Tract 90; that is, in 1841. Yet he knew in 1839 he was preaching principles favourable to Rome, yet tells us (p. 217) he was fighting for the Anglican Church in Oxford. I may admit the being deceived, but I cannot admit it was not deceiving. He charges (p. 87) others as being as bad; but this is a poor defence. I think the only possible excuse is a confusion and self-deception which comes from the enemy.

He says in 1845, when a Romanist, " I

do not think at all more than I did that the Anglican principles which I advocated at the date you mention, lead men to the Church of Rome. If I must specify what I mean by 'Anglican principles,' I should say, *e.g.*, taking *antiquity*, not the *existing Church*, as the oracle of truth" (p. 156). Yet in p. 168 he says, "I recognized, in principles which I had honestly preached . . . conclusions favourable to the cause of Rome. . . . The prime instance of this was the appeal to antiquity."

This confession was the effect of habitual mental dishonesty. I do not now enlarge on Tract 90. Dr. N. has still no consciousness of it. Thus his attempt to show the articles purposely left questions open, and those on which the controversy hinged. Article XII. positively states that good works, which are the fruits of faith, and follow after justification, are pleasing and acceptable to God in Christ; and the XIII., which is—*Of works before Justifi-*

cation, says, "Works done before the grace of Christ and the inspiration of His Spirit are not agreeable to God." Dr. N.'s comment is, "They say that works *before* grace *and* justification are worthless and worse, and that works *after* grace *and* justification are acceptable; but they do not speak at all of works *with* God's aid *before* justification." (p. 86.) They do not, because they say that good works, without any distinction at all, are the fruits of faith, and follow after justification; that is, they say there are not any such. Nor can the miserable plea, that "which" distinguishes some, namely, those that spring from faith, and follow, be of any avail. Not only is it evident to every upright person that it is not the meaning of the sentences, but the title disproves it, and the next article sets it at rest, because it says of works done before justification, "Forasmuch as they spring not from faith in Christ, they are not pleasant to God." He says, " They say that councils called by *princes* may err ; they do not determine whether councils called in the name of Christ may err." To be sure. But they say, general councils (none, that is) cannot be called without the commandment and will of princes ; and that general councils, which cannot be called in any other way, may and have erred.

That is, it applies to all general councils. No ; all this is offensive dishonesty. He was trying, as he says, how much the Church of England could bear ; he did not expect people to look at the articles for themselves. I think his answer to Mr. Kingsley, as to the sermon on "Wisdom and Innocence" being a Pro-. testant sermon, dishonest ; but I will not enter on that part of the book. It is to be noted, that already in 1833, when abroad, he was forming theories which tended to obliterate "the stain upon my imagination" his youth had left as regards Rome. And note, this was not

268 Analysis of Dr. Newman's

merely his feelings, which he tells us all through the book led him Romewards; "but as regards my reason, I began in 1833 to form theories." It was deliberate; it was his reason. Foolish his theories were; but that is not my subject now. It was the *genius loci* like the Prince of Persia, one of his Alexandrian middle demons, neither good nor bad absolutely, which infected "the undeniably most exalted Church in the whole world."

I cannot but think, Dr. N.'s book to prove himself honest, proves distinctly he was not. As to a Protestant theology in the interpretation of the articles, "it sets his teeth on edge even to hear the sound" of it. He had led many on so far towards Popery, that he was forced, when ordered by Dr. Bagot to try and keep them, to stretch the articles as far as possible, without their being aware why, as we have seen him say. Was he honestly asking what they did mean?

Not he; he tells us so: but what they could bear by perversion. "Man had done his worst to disfigure, to mutilate, the old Catholic truth; but there it was, in spite of them, in the articles still." (p. 130.) We have seen how he found it there. It will be said, But his protest against Rome saved his consistency. His consistency in what? Forming theories in favour of it, tenderly loving it, counting it the most exalted Church in the world? But there was no conviction in his protest either. In excusing himself, when he retracted his words against Rome, he tells us, at the time he protested, "I said to myself, I am not speaking my own words; I am but following almost a *consensus* of the divines of my own Church. They have ever used the strongest language against Rome, even the most able and learned of them. I wish to throw myself into their system. While I say what they say, I am safe. Such

views, too, are necessary for our position."
(p. 201.)   Yes, they spoke against Rome,
but they believed what they said.   They
were opposed to Rome.   Dr. N. favoured
it.   He has explained their words when
urged against him; but there is no ex-
plaining them to an honest mind.   I
admit he did not believe in transubstantiation; he thought they adored the Virgin
Mary too much.   But these were slight
things; he joined the Church of Rome
when he did not believe them a bit more.
He believed them because Rome was now
an oracle, and what she taught must be
right.

I do not think I ever met, in all my
experience, a mind so *effœta veri* as Dr.
Newman's, so perfectly incapable of valu-
ing truth; and truth of doctrine has more
to say to truthfulness than we are aware,
for we are sanctified by the truth.   In
that conviction which wholly overthrew
his whole scheme of the *via media*, it

never occurred to him to think, even, whether in one case error was opposed, in the other, truth.

In studying the monophysite history— that is, the controversy whether Christ had one nature or two, or rather, whether the divinity did not take the place of a human soul, he found Eutyches on one side, and Leo, a most able Pope, on the other, who wrote a famous letter, accepted by the Council of Chalcedon as rightly defining the doctrine; and the doctrine so defined has been ever since accepted. Eutyches sought imperial protection : well, here was a Pope instructing a council, and a heretic condemned; the universal Church accepting the council's act. At Trent a Pope confirms a council's decisions, which the Protestant world does not accept; consequently the Protestant world must be as wrong as Eutyches. What the composition of the Council of Trent was; what the doctrine was that was condemned; whether Eutyches held what was contrary to the faith of the Apostles or not; whether Trent condemned the faith of the Apostles or not, is never a subject of his enquiry even. There was a Pope, and a council, and Eutyches; and a council, and a Pope, and half the European world against it, the Greek Church absent. But as in the two cases there was a Pope and a council (whether general or not, even, is a question), half Europe must be wrong, as Eutyches and many Orientals were. The *only* question for Dr. N. was analogy of position. What was condemned was a matter of total indifference to him.

Dr. Newman knows very well that another Pope and another general council condemned a part of this same Council of Chalcedon for all that—what was called the three chapters. But that was no matter; he was on journey to Rome.*   But, as

* His protest was really to avoid getting the credit of being on his way there.

we have seen, when he joined Rome
he did not believe in transubstantiation
more than before. He says, " People say
that the doctrine of transubstantiation is
difficult to believe. I did not believe the
doctrine till I was a Catholic. I had
no difficulty in believing it, as soon as I
believed that the Catholic Roman Church
was the oracle of God, and that she had
declared this doctrine to be part of the
original revelation." Is it possible for
truth to be more absolutely null in a
human mind, or true faith to be more
absent from it ?

Another principle which really led Dr.
Newman to Popery was the doctrine of
development. I will say a word on this.
I deny it absolutely in divine things. In
the human mind there is development. In
the present truth there cannot be, for God
has been revealed. There is no revelation
more, nor meant to be any. Individuals
may learn more and more, but it is there

T

to be learned. The Scriptures give two positive grounds for this—that I am to continue in what I have learned as the only true ground of safety, that I know of whom I have learned them. There is a negative ground of proof—the Apostles committing us, when they should be gone, to that which would be a security for us. If the person of Christ be the foundation truth of Christianity, as Scripture declares it is, as the Son revealing the Father, it is clear there can be no development. His person cannot be developed. But I quite understand it will be said, " Of course not ; but the revelation of it can." Equally impossible. He Himself is wholly, fully revealed, and reveals the Father. The Holy Ghost has revealed, and is the truth.

Hence John, who treats this subject, declares that was to continue (abide in them) which they had learned, and they would so abide in the Father and in the

Son. They could not have more. If any doctrine other than this, or "παρά" (beyond or on one side), besides "what he preached," says Paul, "was preached," neither the doctrine nor the preacher were to be received. If the Church did not possess fully the revelation of the Father in the glorified Son by the Holy Ghost, it did not possess Christ at all, as there revealed. If it did, it could not be added to nor developed. If it did add to it, it falsified Christ. That men speculated about it, and their foolish and irreverent speculations had to be rebuked, repressed, corrected, that is true; but whatever was more than returning to the simplicity of the first revelations, or went beyond its fulness, was pure mischief. Either the Apostles and first Church had a full revelation of Christ, or the Church never was founded on it. If they had, there was no development of it. So of His work. It is complete, or the Church is not saved; was completely revealed, or the Church had not its ground of justification and peace. If it had, there was no development. That much was lost I believe.

The greatest stickler for Church authority does not pretend the Church receives a fresh revelation. He merely says that the Church pronounces on truth as having been revealed. But then there can be no development. Till revelation was complete there were further truths unfolded, but it was by revelation. That once complete, all is closed; and Christianity completes it. The Word of God is fulfilled, completed, says Paul to the Colossians (Col. i. 25). We are to walk in the light, as God is in the light. It was an unction of the Holy One, by which we know all things. "The Spirit," says the Apostle, "searcheth all things, yea, the deep things of God." And then the Apostle tells us he spoke by the Holy

Spirit, in words which He taught (1 Cor. ii. 10–15). The true light now shines. We have the glory of God in the face of Jesus Christ. The Holy Ghost may guard the saints against error, and shew it is error; but the Apostles were guided into all truth. Thus John, in a passage quoted, "Let that therefore abide in you which ye have heard from the beginning. If that which ye have heard from the beginning abide in you, ye also shall continue in the Father and in the Son." We have the glory of God in the face of Jesus Christ. So again: "Continue thou in the things that thou hast learned, knowing of whom thou hast learned them." Paul, in going, commends them to God, and the Word of His grace, as sufficient. Peter writes that they should have, after his decease, these things always in remembrance. As Tertullian justly says, "What is first is the truth." If Eutyches introduces error, Eutyches may be condemned, and truth stated; but that is not development, but maintenance of the truth as it had been revealed.

The Church does not teach; the teacher teaches. The Church abides in and professes the truth she has learned. She is, or ought to be, the pillar and ground of the truth; but she does not teach it. The mystery of iniquity began in the Apostles' days: the last days were already come. *The Truth* was there; but men, like Satan, abode not in it. But abiding in it, walking in it, in the truth perfectly revealed in Christ, that was the duty of the saint, even if the professing Church would not, and the time should come when they would turn away from the truth. Paul declared they would.

In result, Dr. N.'s book presents us with this history—a man who declares that he was converted in a system and by truth which he afterwards gave up.

I value the doctrine of the Church of

God deeply, as the body of Christ (Eph. i.), and on earth the dwelling-place of the Spirit (Eph. ii). I believe the confounding these two to be the source of Popery, and men's present confusions. But I do not believe that trusting the Church is the ground of faith, for then there could have been none. Heathen and Jews did not receive the Church at all. "Of His own will begat He us," says James, "by the word of truth."

However, I am analyzing Dr. N.'s account. He was converted, he is still perfectly sure, at fifteen, by the power of certain truths, and by the instrumentality of a clergyman he calls Calvinistic. He got then and there, in the system he left, conversion, of which he is "still more certain than that he has hands and feet" (p. 4), and the beginning of divine faith, so he calls it now. In a word, he owes his salvation to what he got then. He, indeed, all but admits it was entirely obtained there.

Next we see him gradually giving up the truth which was the means of it, by intercourse with Dr. Hawkins, Froude, Whately, James, and Bishop Butler.* The result has been, that he has *wholly apostatized from all true ground of faith.* " Speaking historically of what I held in 1833–4, I say, that I believed in a God on a ground of probability, that I believed in Christianity on a probability, and that I believed in Catholicism on a probability, and that all these were about the same kind of probability, accumulative, a transcendant probability ; but still probability, inasmuch as He who made us has willed, that, in a religious inquiry, we arrive at certitude by accumulated probabilities."

It was thus he was "led on into the Church of Rome." That is, it was by giving up all true faith. Faith is the reception of a divine testimony by the

---

* [That is, with Bishop Butler's book, *The Analogy of Religion.*—Ed.]

operation of the Spirit of God, and can
have no possible connection with probability. To say it is probable that God
speaks the truth, would be a blasphemy.
He who receives a thing as probable, does
not believe that God has said or taught
it at all. What led Dr. N. to Popery was
giving up faith. In this way he was in a
sick state of soul, neither able to acquiesce
in Anglicanism, nor to go to Rome; but
thought, by some vision first, and then a
special call, as to which he was not quite
sure, but that it came from Satan; he
says, he had a mission, a charge, and was
diligently making converts, until, after
Tract 90, he gave up the lead in the
movement. All the while his heart was
towards Rome: she was certainly Catholic,
he was not quite sure that England was;
at any rate, she needed a complete revolution in her state. As to the true unity
of the body, he never had an idea of it.
He threatened his Romanist friends, and

threatened the Bishops. Knew, as we have seen, at the bottom of his heart, that he was going to Rome; had a secret longing love of it, and knew he was disposing others to it, yet worked on.

The result of his account is this—The truth was the means of his conversion to God; departure from all true ground of faith, that of his going to Rome.

LONDON:
ELLIOT STOCK, PATERNOSTER ROW.

www.ingramcontent.com/pod-product-compliance
Lightning Source LLC
Chambersburg PA
CBHW080550090426
42735CB00016B/3200